Loves
Me
Not

Also by the authors
Sophie's Legacy, 2011

Loves Me Not

How to Keep Relationships Safe

BASED ON THE SOPHIE ELLIOTT
STORY AND WHAT WE MISSED

Lesley Elliott

with William J. O'Brien

RANDOM HOUSE
NEW ZEALAND

A RANDOM HOUSE BOOK published by Random House New Zealand,
18 Poland Road, Glenfield, Auckland, New Zealand

For more information about our titles go to www.randomhouse.co.nz

A catalogue record for this book is available from the
National Library of New Zealand

Random House New Zealand is part of the Random House Group
New York   London   Sydney   Auckland   Delhi   Johannesburg

First published 2014

© 2014 Lesley Elliott with William J. O'Brien

The moral rights of the author have been asserted

ISBN 978 1 77553 600 0
eISBN 978 1 77553 601 7

Design: Carla Sy
Cover illustration: Shutterstock

Printed in China by RR Donnelley Asia Printing Solutions Limited

The paper this book is printed on is certified against the Forest Stewardship
Council® Standards. Griffin Press holds FSC chain of custody certification SGS-
COC-005088. FSC promotes environmentally responsible, socially beneficial and
economically viable management of the world's forests.

Dedication

This book is dedicated to the memory of my beloved daughter Sophie, along with Emily Longley, Christie Marceau, Helen Meads and the other 80 New Zealand women who have died at the hands of a partner or ex-partner in the six years since Sophie lost her life. RIP.

May their legacy encourage us to take a zero tolerance stand on violence, leading to a dramatic reduction in the deaths of women and children.

Contents

Acknowledgements

I agreed to write this book at the request of my publisher, Random House. Initially I thought it was beyond me as I am a nurse and mother — not a trained counsellor. Sophie lived through a five-month-long relationship with a man who would eventually kill her. Because of the close relationship I had with Sophie I effectively lived the relationship also. But despite that, and despite all of the research I have looked at, I would like to make it perfectly clear I am not in any way trained for guidance counselling.

To ensure the information in this book is sound and therefore safe, I sought advice from numerous highly experienced professionals. I am indebted to the following people for their wisdom, expertise and guidance:

Nigel Latta, one of New Zealand's best-known clinical psychologists and commentator on teenagers, for contributing the chapter One for the Boys.

Gayna McConnell, an experienced and respected

school guidance counsellor, for her chapter, Navigating Love.

Although I wrote the sections Online Health Checks and Friends, along with other words of advice, I was only able to do so with the assistance of other guidance counsellors, including Jean Andrews, Heather Knox and Marcelle Nader-Turner. I very much appreciate their wise words.

To ensure this book would stand scrutiny I asked a range of people to review the manuscript independently. Thanks to Marie Norton and Jenny Corlet, school guidance counsellors who have experience as facilitators of the Year 12 workshop Loves-Me-Not. Also Rowan Milburn, assistant principal of a large co-ed school, who led one of the trials of Loves-Me-Not.

For a totally independent set of eyes the manuscript was sent to Graham Gibbs, a former police education officer experienced in programmes such as Keeping Ourselves Safe.

The expertise of all of these people has enabled me to write this book with confidence and I so very much appreciate your help.

I also want to thank Dr Alison Towns for allowing me to use interviews from her research into the Cultures of Cool.

The support of Eric and Sue Faesenkloet enabled me to set the wheels in motion to produce this book and the Zonta Organisation made it possible for the book to be printed and distributed to students. I am indebted to these people. A further acknowledgement to Zonta is included on page 158.

Thanks must also go to the publishers at Random House for their ongoing support of not only me but also the Sophie Elliott Foundation. To Barbara Larson and the team, a big thank you.

Finally I want to thank my co-author, Bill (William J) O'Brien, for his unstinting support of me, the Sophie Elliott Foundation and the anti-violence cause. Bill's inspiration comes from his two young granddaughters who, in a decade from now, will in all likelihood be heading into relationships of their own.

Lesley Elliott, 2014

Preface

In 2008 my daughter Sophie, then aged 22, lost her life at the hands of an ex-partner. During the police investigation it became clear that Sophie's murderer was a typical abuser who had a track record of treating partners badly. Regrettably, none of his partners ever reported his behaviour to the police.

I began to research the phenomenon of domestic and partner abuse and was astonished to find the very characteristics that are evident in abusive relationships were right there in Sophie's. We had simply, through ignorance and naïvety, missed them. I concluded that if both Sophie and I could miss these signs then so too could many other people.

It became apparent that education was the key to recognising the signs of domestic and partner abuse, and therefore preventing it. It was for this reason that I set up the Sophie Elliott Foundation, to raise awareness among all young women and their friends and families to the signs of partner abuse. One of the aims of the foundation was to develop a national secondary school programme that would teach young people about the warning signs and risk factors for abuse, and to equip them with the skills to recognise and get themselves out of unhealthy relationships. It so happened that the New Zealand Police and members of the Ministry of Social Development's It's not OK campaign had a similar vision. Together we formed a partnership and developed the Year 12 workshop Loves-Me-Not.

The idea is for this book to be kept as a reference point. If, at some time in the near or distant future, someone who has taken part in the Loves-Me-Not programme becomes concerned at how their or a friend's relationship is going, they can access this book and refresh their memories as to what should constitute a healthy relationship. This book includes advice and suggestions on how to identify problems, how to deal with them, and where to seek help.

There are a couple of points I need to make, and one is aimed at males. In my situation the psychological then physical violence on Sophie was perpetrated by a man. Of course my story must reflect that. However, this in no way implies that I am anti-male or that what I write is man bashing — it's not. Even though 85 per cent of family violence incidents reported to police are perpetrated by males, I acknowledge that abuse goes both ways, as reinforced by Nigel Latta in his chapter, One for the Boys. But because of size and strength women tend to come off worse. There is no doubt that partner or relationship violence (or whatever name you want to give it) is not okay.

The other point is that this story is about the signs of abuse in a relationship that Sophie and I missed. I'm not suggesting that all or even the majority of relationships are abusive. Sophie also had some lovely experiences with young men who treated her well, as she did them.

I want to share with you a delightful episode I experienced in a large North Island co-ed school. I had been invited to speak to senior students as I have done all over the country. In the front row, sitting together, was a Year 13 girl with her boyfriend. They were holding hands. At one stage she caught my eye and smiled. I knew instantly what she was telling me. She was saying, 'I'm listening to your advice, Lesley, but this doesn't apply to us. We treat each other really well.' I found out later they were indeed a lovely and loving couple. I wish them well and hope neither ever sees the signs of an unhealthy relationship that I talk of. But if either of them ever does I'm sure they will have the skills to cope.

Please read this book and reflect on the messages, and join me in renouncing any form of violence. It isn't necessary and we don't want it.

I have written this book in memory of my beloved daughter Sophie. While I hope none of you ever finds yourself in an unhealthy relationship, I trust that you will find the advice in this book of some use.

Lesley Elliott, Chair, Sophie Elliott Foundation
www.sophieelliottfoundation.co.nz

Introduction

I knew that Wednesday 9 January 2008 was going to be a day of mixed emotions. I was helping my daughter Sophie with her final packing before she shifted north to Wellington to take up her first full-time job after finishing university. She had secured a position at Treasury as a graduate analyst and, like her, I was excited at the prospects this job offered. But this excitement was also tinged with sadness.

Sophie was my youngest child and only daughter. Her two brothers, Chris, seven years older, and Nick, 11 years older, had already left home to make their way in the world and were living in Melbourne and Sydney respectively. There was no doubt I was going to miss Sophie terribly. With two boys in Australia and my husband managing the medical diagnostic laboratory at Dunstan Hospital some 200 kilometres away, Sophie and I had become more than mother and daughter. We were also friends who shared an extremely close bond and the next day she would be on her way to Wellington, leaving me very much alone. But our cherished time together was soon to be shattered in the cruellest way imaginable.

Our home, nestled into a peaceful setting atop a hill and surrounded by beautiful trees and shrubs, overlooks Dunedin Harbour. The day was gorgeous, the sort of day to really lift one's spirits. We were up early and I helped Sophie make some semblance of order in her bedroom. There were clothes everywhere. While she got on with packing her clothing, I wrapped fragile things — mirrors, her television set and the like — and boxed them up. Together we carried the full cartons downstairs ready for the removal men who were coming later. Sophie was dressed in a denim miniskirt, white shirt and short-sleeved white cardigan. She looked lovely, as she always did. At one stage I walked past her bedroom door and noticed her putting on make-up. 'Are you going out?' I asked. Sophie had a reputation for being late but on this occasion, her last chance to be with her closest friends, she wanted to be on time for a pizza together at the beach later that day. She knew with all the packing ahead she should take the chance to get ready, even if the meeting was hours away. She looked up and said something endearing, though I can't for the life of me recall what it was. However, it was enough to bring me to tears. Sophie asked me what was wrong and I told her I was going to miss her so much. She said she would come home to visit regularly and had even arranged to be here for Easter. She came over and gave me a big hug. That was to be the last hug we shared.

A while later I was in the kitchen having just listened to the midday news on the radio. There was a knock at the door. I looked out the window and couldn't see a car in the drive so peered around to see her former boyfriend, Clayton Weatherston, standing there. I was surprised as he had always parked in the driveway before. I opened the door cautiously. He had a grin on his face. 'Is Sophie in? I have something for her.' Sophie had heard the knock and was on the upper landing. She mouthed down to me, 'Who is it?' I mouthed back that it was Clayton. She shrugged her shoulders and raised her eyes to the ceiling but continued coming down the stairs. I opened the door wider and he came in. I didn't hear what he said but I remember Sophie saying she was really busy and running late. If he wanted to talk it would have to be in her room while she completed her packing. I returned to the kitchen. Remembering his recent assaults on Soph, I began to shake. I wondered what I should do. Sophie's bedroom is directly above the kitchen and normal conversation can be heard as faint murmuring, with any raised voices heard easily. I felt apprehensive and instinctively turned off the radio. I didn't want to interfere as I knew Sophie would be angry with me. I listened but couldn't hear anything, not even a murmur. Soon after I heard the bathroom door close and Sophie appeared in the kitchen. I said, 'What's going on?' She said, 'I don't know what he wants. He's just sitting there not saying a word.' I told her to get rid of him as she was running late and had heaps to do before going out. I suggested that maybe he just wanted to make amends over the assaults and ensure she wasn't going to report him to the police. The toilet flushed and Sophie said I was probably right and she would get him to go. She went up the stairs and I heard the door close. This was followed by a terrible scream.

I don't think there is anything to be gained by detailing what happened next, certainly not for this book; suffice to say that this man's attack on Sophie was brutal and her death, and the ensuing court cases spread over the next 20 months, literally shocked the nation. If people want or need to know more it is all documented in my book *Sophie's Legacy*. For the purposes of this book I am more interested in providing advice on what I have since learned about the signs of an abusive relationship. I am motivated by what happened to Sophie so that more young people will not fall into the insidious trap of abusive and manipulative relationships. I hope that what I say from here on might help you and those close to you avoid a lot of heartache.

CHAPTER 1

Who Was
Sophie Elliott?

Before I get into the signs we missed, I want to share a little bit about Sophie, because when you really look at her, she was no different to most other young people.

One thing I do want to emphasise is that Sophie and I had an extremely close relationship, which perhaps isn't typical between mother and daughter. In fact she used to confide in me to the extent I'd often say, 'Too much information, Soph.' To this she would smile and say, 'I know,' then do a bit of a twirl around the dining room. On reflection I think she was trying to bait me and I never quite rose to it. Also, on reflection, I now appreciate how valuable our understanding was. I hope that when young people find the going tough they will confide in their parents more.

Sophie had one long-term boyfriend who she went flatting with after they had been together for a couple of years. Less than a year later they seemed to grow apart and eventually broke up. Sophie came back home while she finished her university studies. With my two sons living in Australia and my husband working in Central Otago, this left just me and Sophie at home. She would remark, 'It's like we're flatting together, isn't it?' I used to think to myself, *Sure it is, but how come I seem to do all the work?* Still, I loved having her about.

For the most part she was fun-loving, bright, intelligent and witty. Above all, she was caring, and perhaps this is what ultimately led to her downfall. Sophie never wanted an enemy. If she and a boyfriend broke up she still wanted to remain friends. I believe this is why she kept giving Weatherston another chance. She was too forgiving of the way he treated her and spoke to her. He would say, 'Don't I get another chance?' and she would relent. She often said to me, 'I have to see if this will work,' even though I can see now it was never going to. But that was the caring, forgiving nature of Sophie. If she was your girlfriend and you had an argument, she would be the first to text and say, 'Can we meet for coffee?'

I just want to give you a quick snapshot of the Sophie I loved and admired. I do so to show that what happened to Sophie could happen to any young person.

So who was Sophie Kate Elliott?

There was nothing extraordinary about Sophie. She grew up the same as most New Zealand kids. She absolutely loved dancing and was very active in pursuits like ice skating and tennis. In her later teens she became motivated to do well at anything she put her mind to. She had a great circle of friends she loved to socialise with and she remained loyal to them. Sophie not only worked hard at university, she supported herself by working at night in a video rental store and every weekend at a Spectrum Photos processing store. She was very passionate about photography. So she certainly packed a lot into her life.

Sophie had a bright and bubbly personality, but also a single-minded and determined drive about her. She kept fit at the gym and always seemed to be in a hurry. The mother of one of Sophie's friends used to say that even when Soph was standing still it was like she was idling — ready to take off to something else.

Academically Sophie achieved well. She was *proxime accessit* at her college and achieved first class honours in economics at Otago University. But that success didn't come easily and she worked extremely hard to get her results. One of the most heart-breaking but proudest moments I have ever had was to see Sophie's brother accept her degree in Dunedin's town hall some months after she had died. Her efforts were acknowledged by the standing ovation of staff, students and the public.

So Sophie was in many respects just like any other young person with ambitions and dreams. She was a good friend and a loving daughter and sister.

There are many Sophies out there. I know through my work with the Sophie Elliott Foundation that many lives have been lost, damaged or inhibited by manipulative, controlling partners, both male and female. Only with hindsight do I see Sophie's situation so clearly now. I firmly believe education is the key and if only Sophie had a workshop such as Loves-Me-Not when she was at high school, things might have been so different.

In the following pages I've written about some of

the typical behaviours of abusers and the warning signs of an unhealthy relationship, things that Sophie and I missed. What I have written here isn't rocket science. In fact it all looks blindingly obvious. But the reality is that these signs get overlooked time after time. The first part of the book discusses character traits of abusers and common scenarios found in unhealthy relationships. I've illustrated these with the signs I've since found in Sophie's relationship with Clayton Weatherston. Following this is a chapter written by counsellor Gayna McConnell that includes lots of great advice about how to establish healthy relationships and communicate well with a partner. There are scenarios to talk about and ways to understand your own strengths and weaknesses. Clinical psychologist Nigel Latta has contributed a chapter, where he talks about how abuse affects not just girls and women but boys and men too.

I want to again make it clear that I am not a counsellor or trained in this area at all. I'm simply a nurse and a mum with a story to tell.

CHAPTER 2

Power and Control

I had only heard the name Clayton Weatherston a couple of times and was somewhat surprised when Sophie said she was going to go out with him. Weatherston was a tutor at Otago University and took one of Sophie's economic honours classes. My immediate reaction was rather negative and Sophie asked why. I said it was all to do with professional boundaries.

I am a nurse and nurse–patient relationships are forbidden as are doctor–patient ones. Lawyers can't go out with clients and teacher–pupil relationships are strictly forbidden. As Weatherston's student, Sophie was in direct contact with him three days a week. Of course I was concerned, but Sophie said he knew the university's ethical behaviour policy and all he had to do was declare the liaison so the situation could be managed. He did do this, though I've got to say he took his time over it, despite his office being only a few doors along from the head of department's.

I never fully appreciated just how difficult it would be for other students in a class if one of them is dating their tutor. Imagine all of the students being marked by one person while Sophie was marked by another. What are the implications? It could be that Sophie's marker could be more generous, meaning she would get better marks. Conversely the marker might be stricter, therefore Sophie would be disadvantaged. Either way, it's not fair. Others in the class might feel Sophie was getting preferential treatment, perhaps believing that Weatherston would tell her what might be in an exam paper.

The way this situation was managed was that Sophie's work was set and graded by an independent marker. Sophie told me that Weatherston didn't appear to like that. I believe he wanted to have a degree of control over Sophie's future, a typical trait of an abuser. He couldn't make her a better student, as she was already achieving at an A+ level. However, several incidents during their rocky relationship led me to believe he tried to fail her.

I recall an episode that Sophie told me about, where she asked him a question about a topic she was studying. He replied, 'Don't worry about it,' from which Sophie took to mean it wouldn't be in an exam so what was the point of studying it. As it turned out the topic was in a paper — and worth a significant mark. On reflection I think he was deliberately deceiving her.

Any thoughts that Weatherston might be giving

Sophie preferential treatment were dispelled in my mind fairly early on. One day Sophie came home complaining about him. 'What's the use of having a boyfriend who tutors in a subject but won't help me?' I asked her what she meant and she said that when she was at his flat she would ask him a question and he would shout at her, things like: 'Why don't you listen in class?' or 'Why don't you read the textbook?' Subsequently I have learned that he wasn't quite as bright as he made out and perhaps he simply didn't know the answers to the questions.

The five-month relationship Sophie had with Weatherston was on-again, off-again. Because I do shift work there were times I wouldn't see Sophie for a few days. We had a standing joke. When I did see her I would say, 'Well, what is it this week, is it on or off?' She might say it's off and she would never see him again. The next week she might come home and say, 'You're not going to be pleased but he wants me to give him another chance.'

This concerned me in relation to the make-up of Sophie's class. Being an honours group there were only eight students. They had been together for half a year and gelled really well. The class worked hard and socialised together so they certainly had a bond. The difficulty for Sophie's fellow honours students was that when the relationship was on there was giggling and silly carryings-on, but when it was off there were snide remarks and a cold atmosphere. In a conversation I had with Sophie's supervisor some time after she died, he told me that a group of students came to him wanting help. When he asked them why they hadn't asked Mr Weatherston they said it was because he was strange and creepy, and when they put their hands up in computer labs he often wouldn't come to them. It was then they raised the matter of a girl in class (meaning Sophie) who was sitting alone and distressed. It must have been a very difficult time emotionally for Sophie, who had to sit in a class where she was being tutored by someone with whom she had had a falling out.

I mention these things because you should be careful about forming a relationship with someone who has power and control over you, for instance, in a work situation. Imagine working part-time in a supermarket. You become attracted to a supervisor and you start dating him or her. That's probably fine while things are going well. But what might happen if the relationship turns sour? I'm not saying 'don't do it' — I am saying think about the possible repercussions of going out with someone who can influence your life. I saw this kind of power imbalance in Sophie's relationship and it concerns me even more now than it did at the time.

Age difference — does it matter?

In my opinion age difference does matter. Not for a moment am I suggesting that having a partner older than you is inappropriate or in some way dangerous. What I am saying is that research suggests that if the older partner is prone to abusive behaviour then the age difference is an important consideration. And that same research points to a 10-year age difference as being particularly significant. Interestingly, Weatherston was 32, a decade older than Sophie.

Another interesting fact revealed during the police investigation was that Weatherston had boasted of having many girlfriends prior to Sophie, somewhere around 25. Conversely, Sophie had had three or four boyfriends, one long-term. All had treated her well. Curiously, all of Weatherston's girlfriends that I found out about were around 10 years younger than him.

Was it his immaturity that attracted him to younger women, or was it that older women saw through him? I'm sure that if Sophie was 32 at the time she went out with him she simply wouldn't have put up with his antics and behaviour. With life experience she would have been far less accepting. And that is essentially the key — experience.

My advice is that if you are in a relationship with an older person, especially if the age difference is 10

years or more, just be careful. If there are elements
of control in the relationship they will be harder
to deal with if one partner is vastly less mature or
experienced than the other.

❁ Think twice about starting a
relationship with someone who can
hold some sort of power and control
over your life. This might be someone
older, or your supervisor at work.

❁ Having a relationship with someone
who can influence you can leave you
isolated from your peers, and at the
whim of your partner's moods.

❁ Make sure any professional
boundaries are observed, and
those higher up know about the
relationship.

CHAPTER 3

Communication

In this age of such
rapid technological
advances the issue of
communication is more
important than ever.
There are so many
mediums available,
such as texting, cameras
on mobile phones,
Facebook, Twitter and
phone apps, all making
communication easier
and convenient, but also
incredibly dangerous.
I believe we all need to
think carefully about
how we access modern
communication systems
because nothing is safe
or secure once you 'put
it out there'.

Confusing communication

In Sophie's case most communication was done by email or text. While she was a texter, Weatherston certainly wasn't, which is somewhat curious. In many respects he fitted the classic abuser model, but one thing he didn't do was text incessantly. In fact, quite the opposite. I'm told by people who work in the domestic abuse field that many abusive partners text non-stop. They want to know where you are, who you are with, what you are wearing, where you are going next, etcetera, etcetera. In Weatherston's case he would reply to texts when he felt like it or when it suited him. He didn't have a landline in his flat, meaning Sophie's only chance to communicate with him was when he was in his office at the university or by mobile phone. She used to get annoyed with his lack of response at times.

An example would be making plans for Friday night. Sophie would text him during the day to ask, 'What are we doing tonight?' If it didn't suit him he simply wouldn't reply. However, a text or call might come through at 11pm, by which time Sophie had either decided to go to bed or had gone out with her girlfriends. Of course, if he did want to go out he would make contact and expect Sophie to drop everything (including assignments) to be at his beck and call. In hindsight I see his communication style was designed to keep Sophie dangling and she confided in me that this caused her confusion. When they went out socialising, Sophie was invariably the sober driver, therefore she would drop him off at his flat. When he got out of the car he would say to Sophie, 'I'll leave it up to you to contact me.' This is where further confusion came in. Sophie didn't know whether he wanted to go out with her or not. My belief now is that this behaviour was arrogance fuelled by the narcissistic personality he was later diagnosed with. A narcissist is basically a person who has an exceptional interest and admiration for themselves. I think he just enjoyed the thought that an attractive young woman would happily chase after him.

This whole dynamic between him and Sophie, while it was confusing and annoying for her, has certainly intrigued me since and made me think a lot about how we communicate with boyfriends and girlfriends. When I speak to groups of young people I ask, how do you communicate? Is it random and is it always left to you to initiate the contact? If so, then maybe you need to think about whether you really want to be in the relationship. If it's not equal then is it a healthy relationship?

Your words can be used against you

I want to sound out a word of warning about modern systems of communication. When things go seriously wrong in a relationship and it ends up in court, everything can be up for grabs — your mobile phone conversations, emails, Facebook entries and diaries — absolutely everything. In Sophie's case she kept an electronic diary, one that she wrote for her eyes only. It was the sort of diary where you might expect a young woman to detail her innermost thoughts and emotions. A diary of the type that is helpful for young people trying to figure out what feels right and what feels wrong, what is good and what is bad. Diaries are a great way to crystallise our thinking as we negotiate our way through the emotional minefield life can be, especially for a girl in search of womanhood. The entries were for Sophie alone — not for the world to see.

After Sophie died the police used their electronic crime laboratory to get into her diaries to see if there were any leads relating to their investigation. Of course they had to disclose this to the defence. The criminal justice system favours the rights of the accused so the defence team had to be given access to Sophie's diaries. And that means, through them, her murderer also got access to her thoughts. I can't accept that. Perhaps I could understand the reasoning if the defence only had the entries covering the five months of the relationship, but why should Weatherston and his lawyers be given access to what Sophie wrote for the three or four years before she met him? I don't believe that's fair. And I abhor the way a single entry can be taken out of context and used to darken Sophie's character. I'll give one such example.

Sophie had been in a long-term relationship with a young man she had met at high school. I can't use his name because there is a name suppression order still in force and I don't intend to be in contempt of court. They met each other through a mutual interest in drama and when he wanted a partner for a school formal Sophie went with him. The friendship flourished and they went out together for some time, eventually becoming partners. They lived in our home with us for about a year and we got on well. When they finally moved into a flat of their own they seemed settled and happy. Both he and Sophie were intelligent, strong-willed young people. If something caused a disagreement they would both stand their ground and argue the point. One night they did have a heated exchange and Sophie accidentally scratched his neck. It was no big deal, but Sophie was mortified and in tears. She hadn't meant to do it and regretted it immediately. She recorded this in her diary. When Weatherston was arrested and during the following 20 months he never once mentioned that Sophie had attacked him. But at his trial he claimed she came at him with scissors. The defence's line was that Sophie was prone to attacking boyfriends who annoyed her, therefore she could easily have attacked Weatherston in her bedroom following what the defence claimed was an argument over Sophie not liking Weatherston's mother. Sophie's bedroom is directly above the kitchen. Even if she and Weatherston were talking normally I would have heard them. An argument would have certainly registered with me.

Sophie's long-term boyfriend wasn't called as a witness but his name was mentioned in the carefully selected diary entry. Later on he told me about the scratch. He said that he and Sophie got into a verbal argument with him going on and on at her, even making a rather vile comment about one of her friends. He certainly wasn't surprised when Sophie lashed out after several hours of being harangued, and after she did she was desperately sorry. The image of Sophie attacking anyone just because she was angry is very hurtful to us. That was not the Sophie we or her former boyfriend knew. But that is the sort of young woman the defence would have you believe Sophie was. I have read the full diary entry Sophie wrote about this incident, and can say that the defence were careful to only produce the part of the entry that showed Sophie in the light they wanted her to be portrayed. It really is unfair.

I give this example to show you that anything you write down, even electronically, can be used in court. I have a lawyer friend who says to young people, you should never record anything you wouldn't want a future mother-in-law to read. And that's sensible advice. We probably think things deleted from a computer or mobile phone are gone forever.

However, at the police electronic crime laboratory almost anything is retrievable.

Communicating online

This advice also applies when you're talking to people online. I think in many ways young people simply aren't ready for some of the websites and social media platforms that are available. I've heard of people posting details about themselves on websites, and inviting others to make comments about them. In their naïvety they expect people will post glowing remarks, but they become devastated when the feedback they read is less than complimentary, sometimes even vile.

Similarly I implore you to take care with pictures. Almost everyone today has access to a phone with a built-in camera. The latest smartphones have cameras capable of taking incredibly detailed photographs. You might be tempted to send a photo to a 'friend' who then thinks it great fun to forward it on to another so-called friend who casually photoshops your photo to become something more compromising and posts that on Facebook. My advice is simple. Be careful how you record your thoughts, words and images. Once a picture or your words go out electronically they are out there forever and you can lose complete control over who sees it and how it is used.

Online health checks

Our physical health is important to us. All of us are told to look for changes in moles and freckles to avoid melanoma or detect it early. Advice for younger people encourages them to eat a balanced diet, to get enough sleep and exercise and to make good decisions around sexual health. But do we ever hear of people doing online health checks?

When Sophie was alive I didn't think that internet bullying was a serious concern. It certainly is now. I feel it is important to talk about healthy online relationships here because it appears that the internet and all the devices we now use to communicate with have become potentially damaging to young people in relationships. Consider this scenario:

Annabelle was looking forward to celebrating her upcoming sixteenth birthday with her close circle of friends. Shane, her boyfriend, was planning a particular surprise and delighted in teasing her as to what it might be. Annabelle was flattered by the attention Shane was giving her but he was annoying in his persistence that she send him a photo of her breasts. She resisted and resisted, but not wanting to appear uncool (and realising she had something to show off) she finally relented. What harm could it do? If she sent it as a Snapchat it would be there for just ten

seconds then gone. Unbeknown to Annabelle,
when the photo came through Shane saw
it along with a group of his mates. On a
borrowed phone he photographed the image
so he could have a lasting picture.

Shane and Annabelle had a big bust up on
the night of her birthday and the relationship
broke up. Annabelle then moved on to a
new and fabulous boyfriend. He had a great
circle of friends among whom Annabelle felt
comfortable. Their relationship was going
well and becoming quite serious until the
bombshell struck — 18 months after breaking
up with Shane the photo of Annabelle
exposing her breasts appeared on a
Facebook page. Annabelle was horrified and
distraught. As the image circulated among
her peer group hateful comments flooded
in. One said: 'You're nothing but a fat, lazy
slut who's slept with everybody. Why don't
you do us all a favour and do away with
yourself.' Annabelle had no way of deleting
any of the comments or the picture.

With the expansion of online media the risks have
become greater. Perhaps the worst thing is not the
technology but the people using it. Some people take
on a different persona online. While they can be nice
to your face, behind a computer screen they can turn
quite vicious. Anonymity allows this to happen. Online
communication can also be a bit like alcohol in that it

can be disinhibiting. People will say things online that they would never say face to face.

You can be more easily bullied and tortured by an ex or their peer group. Unfortunately you can't shut the door on this kind of harrassment. And even more of a concern is that anything you post online can be there FOREVER. Future partners could see posts years later and even prospective employers could uncover things from your past that you would prefer weren't there.

Perhaps ask yourself, when I do find the love of my life, will I be happy with him or her seeing my Facebook page of today?

I'm not an expert in this field, and if you are suffering online pressure or bullying there are experts and organisations, such as NetSafe, that you can go to for help. I just want to get you to think about the issues and take some control. Perhaps you could talk to the adult you consider an ally. Alternatively you might think a complaint to Facebook could help. In serious cases you could consult the police.

The number of social media sites seems to be increasing rapidly. Some are well-established while others come and go. I don't expect this to change, so I would urge young people to regard an online health check seriously.

What would your online health check look like? What would it say about you? Do you accept negative comments about yourself? And do you have 'friends', with access to your page, who you don't know well enough to share private information with?

If you have hundreds of friends on your Facebook

page does it mean you are really popular? Or does it mean hundreds of people know a lot of personal stuff about you? If so, is this safe? Do you accept people into your friends group you don't know? What do you really know about the people you are talking to online? Do you know their character? Do you receive inappropriate texts and pictures with strong sexual overtones, and if so, do you find these flattering?

I don't underestimate the pressures young people face in this increasingly technological world. Even older people, some with responsible jobs and lots of life experience, get ripped off by communicating with people they have never met.

So what can you do? What are the steps you can take rather than leaving things until it is too late? Doing nothing isn't a realistic option and will more likely leave you feeling as bad or worse.

Below some young people have shared the ways they overcame internet bullying. They looked at areas in their lives where they had been strong and applied that strength to their online health check. Some of them asked themselves the following questions:

HOW AM I FEELING WHEN READING MY FACEBOOK PAGE?

IS IT BUILDING UP MY SELF-ESTEEM OR PULLING ME DOWN?

ARE THE 'FRIENDS' WHO ARE CAUSING THE ONLINE PROBLEM WITH NEGATIVE COMMENTS REALLY FRIENDS?

AREN'T FRIENDS SUPPOSED TO BUILD ME UP, AND DO THEY?

DO I HAVE TO RESPOND TO ONLINE COMMENTS OR CAN I RESIST THE TEMPTATION AND JUST IGNORE THEM?

Following is a list of tactics these same people used when they were getting hate messages online. They include:

- ✿ Taking a Facebook holiday. This doesn't mean pulling the plug forever — just taking a break.
- ✿ Turning your phone, laptop, tablet or computer off.
- ✿ Not responding to comments that are getting heavy and, if challenged by others as to why you are not responding, saying parents have

blocked access (if you need an out).
✿ Talking to an adult.
✿ Getting advice from people who know about internet bullying, such as NetSafe.
✿ In serious cases making a complaint to the police.

If a question, photo or comment that you don't like comes through Facebook, Ask.fm, Twitter or anything else, you can choose to bin it. You can give yourself permission to do that. You can take control and make strong choices.

✿ Is there too much or too little communication in your relationship? In a healthy relationship you and your partner should be able to communicate equally.
✿ If you are always intiating the communication then maybe you need to think about whether this is a relationship you want to be in.
✿ Random communication can be used by an abuser to confuse you, and make you unsure of whether they really like you or not.
✿ Be aware that anything you write down can be taken out of context

and out of your control.
❀ Communicating online can be
instant and anonymous.
❀ Whatever you say or post can be
forwarded to others in a second, and
will be around forever.
❀ Make sure you communicate online
only with people you know well
and trust.

CHAPTER 4

Threats and Entitlements

Threats and entitlements
are some of the most
classic warning signs of
an abusive relationship.
Often these behaviours
are quite subtle and may
be misconstrued, but can
go on to become quite
dominant traits.

Entitlement — it's all about them

If someone feels entitled they believe they are deserving of special treatment. Typically entitlement is motivated by selfishness and is characterised by a lack of empathy, or being unable to consider someone else's feelings or situation. On their own, behaviours associated with entitlement may seem almost inconsequential, but collectively they might point to a pattern of behaviour. I'll give you a couple of small examples.

Very early on in their relationship, Sophie invited Weatherston over to our home. I had at this stage only just met him. I can remember Sophie making a cup of a new herbal tea I'd just bought. We shared a cup and then, after a while, he got up and helped himself to another cup. In most cases visitors ask if they want something; that's the social norm. Of course he could have had another cup, but to just go and help yourself in the home of someone you hardly know isn't exactly normal. In hindsight I see this was one of his entitlement traits.

Another example indicates the selfish trait of putting yourself first. Sophie was over at his place one night. The two of them were studying, Sophie for her honours degree and Weatherston for his PhD. It was late and they were feeling hungry so decided to go down to the local supermarket which was open 24/7. Sophie had a basket into which they placed some items of food and he also put in a few toiletries he needed. When they got to the checkout he simply took the toiletries from the basket and went to another checkout, leaving Sophie to pay for the food. Remember that he was in paid employment and had been working for years; she was a student with a weekend job to get herself through varsity. I mention this incident because it illustrates the selfish nature of abusers, and how what you may think are insignificant actions, or nothing to worry about, are part of a larger pattern of behaviour.

Lack of empathy is another strong indicator of entitlement. Abusers care little about how their partner feels. This can be demonstrated to a small degree in an incident where Weatherston and Sophie were out socialising. They were walking back to the car on a particularly cold night and Sophie commented how cold it was. He said to her, 'I'd lend you my jacket but then I'd get cold.' Perhaps it's my old-fashioned idea of chivalry, but when Sophie told me this, I was surprised he didn't lend her his jacket. I think the point here is that if he had no intention of comforting her he'd have been better off saying nothing. Even that small example shows that with Weatherston it was 'all about me'. Where there is a lack of empathy or other indications of your partner putting themselves first, my advice is to seriously start thinking about the relationship you are heading into. A healthy relationship should be equal, not one-sided.

If you find your partner is only concerned about themselves, doesn't care about your wellbeing or is jealous of the things you have, your friends or your career then perhaps they have a sense of entitlement.

Jealousy is another common trait that appears with entitlement. Again this comes down to the abuser believing it's all about them. I can recall a couple of incidents that Sophie shared with me regarding Weatherston's jealousy. One that springs to mind was education. More than once he told her she was lucky she went to a decile 10 school, whereas he had to go to a decile 6. To me that seems a pointless jealousy. And he was dux of his high school so you would wonder why he felt disadvantaged. It doesn't really matter what decile school you go to. Anyone who wants to make it in the world still has to work hard. For an adult in their thirties, their boyfriend or girlfriend's school status shouldn't be a major problem, but Weatherston thought it mattered a lot.

A more obvious example was to do with Sophie's car. We bought our three kids their first cars, just to get them started. Nothing flash, mind you; in fact they could be described as 'bombs', albeit bombs that got warrants. If they wanted something better they were expected to save up for it, and they did. Sophie had a reasonable car — she certainly liked it. Weatherston had a rather clapped-out Toyota, and he showed quite intense jealousy towards Sophie because we had bought her a car, when he had to drive a wreck. Her response was to tell him to buy himself a decent car; after all, he was in full-time employment.

If you find your partner is only concerned about themselves, doesn't care about your wellbeing or is jealous of the things you have, your friends or your career then perhaps they have a sense of entitlement. Should a relationship be one-sided, with one partner given special treatment, or should you each be treated equally?

Threats

Threats can be physical or emotional and aimed at you or your family or pets. Typically abusers will use subtle threats as a form of control, to make their partner comply with their wishes. Perhaps the most common emotional threat is 'If you like or love me you will . . .' Another is 'I will leave you if you don't . . .' This is basically a type of coercion. Often the theme of these threats is that you'll comply with their sexual demands even if you're uncomfortable with what they're asking you to do or you're not ready to take that step in your relationship. A young person in a new relationship is in it because there's an attraction. Not wanting to be rejected, they often give in to the 'If you love me you'll . . .' It can be extremely hard to resist that kind of pressure, and abusers use this tactic to suit their own needs.

Another time threats may be used is with alcohol or drugs. You may not want to drink or take drugs, but peer pressure and wanting to please your partner may see you give in. I don't underestimate how difficult it might be to say no, but my advice is try not to be pulled into the traps that these situations present.

A more difficult scenario to cope with is when your partner tries to make you responsible for their behaviour: 'If you don't do . . . I will . . .', and the most common threat here is to commit suicide. This can be a hugely difficult predicament for a young person to find themselves in. You don't know if the threat is real and you certainly don't want it on your conscience if a person does go ahead and attempt self-harm or suicide because you didn't comply with what they were asking. As I've said, I'm not a counsellor, just a mum telling a story. So what I advise you to do here is take some positive action and seek help from someone you can confide in.

If you don't want to confide in someone, stand strong and be true to yourself. I'd love to hear a young person respond to 'If you love me you will . . .' with 'If you love me you won't pressure me to do that.'

The first time I heard the name Clayton Weatherston was when I was helping Sophie prepare for a trip to Wellington. She had interviews scheduled with the Ministry for Economic Development, the Reserve Bank and Treasury. I offered to go and support her in the evenings. She was grateful that she would have company, although I was in no way involved in the interviews. When I was preparing for our four days away Sophie mentioned that her tutor had offered to go to Wellington with her. I thought, how odd; why would a tutor take a week off work to accompany a student to interviews? Sophie, however, thought it was a nice gesture and believed he genuinely went way beyond the call of duty to help his students. It turned out that Weatherston had worked at Treasury some years before but his tenure hadn't lasted long. He told Sophie he had returned to Dunedin due to homesickness, but I have since learned that his narcissistic personality simply wasn't tolerated. I have also become aware of him taking unkindly to being reprimanded at Treasury. Sophie, being offered the job he had once aspired to, was something he could not accept and I believe he may have tried to sabotage her success had he gone with her, by further undermining her confidence.

Just a few months into their relationship Weatherston made a direct threat. One day Sophie came home from university in floods of tears. I was hanging washing on the line and I can still picture her telling me that he was going to ruin her career at Treasury. I said, how can he? She replied that Weatherston had said he was going to contact his 'friends' at Treasury and tell them what a f***ing awful person she was and to not have anything to do with her. She was convinced that he would do this and it took an effort to get Sophie to see sense. In the end I had to shout at her, something I seldom did. She stopped crying and I said, 'Soph, he was at Treasury about six or seven years ago and didn't last long. So who does he know there — probably no one? It's just a jealous threat. Go to Treasury, be yourself and do the job you know you can do and if anyone asks, do you know this man?, just say he was a tutor at uni.' She stopped crying, looked at me and said, 'You're right.'

The thing that disturbed me was that Sophie was an extremely bright and level-headed young woman. Yet she actually believed him. She really thought he had the ability to seriously affect her working life. Something I implore young people in a relationship to do is to keep things in perspective. Ask people you trust what they think about a situation or criticism. I'm still quite astounded at how Sophie believed so many things this man said about her.

Sophie very rarely cried but during her relationship with Weatherston it became increasingly more frequent. I put a lot of it down to the stress she was under completing a heavy academic year, but now

I realise a lot of it was because she had difficulty rationalising her relationship with this man.

The other incident I want to share is what I call the frost incident. As mentioned earlier, Sophie had previously been in a long-term relationship, and when it ended she moved back home. We established some rules, and one in particular I was strict on. I valued my independence and privacy while at the same time respected Sophie's. If Sophie was having someone over to stay I wanted to know. She was an adult in her early twenties so there was no way I wanted to inhibit her life. At the same time I didn't want to come out of my bedroom in the morning to find some stranger wandering around. Sophie entirely respected these arrangements and we agreed that if anyone was staying over she would text or phone me.

On this particular night I was working the night-shift. It's my habit to go to bed after dinner, have a couple of hours sleep, then get up about 10pm so I can be at the hospital ready to start at 11. I knew Weatherston was coming over and they were going to watch a DVD in her room. I'd only met him briefly once before. As I left home I knocked on her bedroom door and said, 'I'm off to work, see you tomorrow.' It was a frosty night and the hill we live on does take a bit of negotiating to get down. But people do it safely every day, and anyone who lives in Dunedin learns to deal with these conditions. When I finished duty at 7am I drove home and again I had to be careful on the icy road, but still handled the conditions easily. When I got home Weatherston's car was still in the driveway.

I was not at all pleased. Truth be known I probably had steam coming out my ears. Sophie could quite easily have sent me a text to say he was staying over and that would have been the end of the matter.

Sophie's bedroom is above the kitchen so I clanged about as loudly as I could, but no one appeared. I duly went off to bed. I always get up at lunchtime after working the nightshift and when I arose his car was still there. By now I had fire coming out my ears.

This was most unusual for Sophie. I swear that girl had 26 hours in the day; she packed so much into her life. If she was in bed after 9am she'd wasted half the day. Also it was a weekday and she usually didn't miss lectures, so why was she still at home?

I was back in the kitchen banging around as loudly as I could and soon after she appeared at the doorway with a finger to her lips, indicating not to speak. Moments later Weatherston appeared but stood in the slightly darker hallway. After a fleeting hello she hurriedly ushered him out and he left. As Sophie came in the door she said, 'Don't be mad, I've got an explanation. He said he couldn't go home as he couldn't drive on ice. I couldn't make him go, Mum, because if he'd had an accident it would be my fault.' While he never directly told Sophie it would be her fault, he certainly inferred it — and she got the message loud and clear. He was indirectly threatening her by making her take responsibility for any consequences.

So what do I take from this incident? It might seem like a trivial matter, but there are a number of things that now make me realise this was a real red flag. The first thing is that this was only three weeks into their relationship and already Sophie's patterns and habits were changing. It was very unusual for her to miss a class. Second, he put a guilt trip on Sophie to get his own way. To compound things, Sophie told me that she didn't want him to stay, but he was insistent he couldn't go — he won. What I've decided since is that he was abusing Sophie. Abusing her kind nature and putting the guilt for any consequences on her. Worse still, he was abusing me. I've no doubt whatsoever that Sophie would have told him what my usual routine was, especially that I got up at midday. He could have had the decency to be gone during the morning.

I use this anecdote to describe the sense of entitlement abusers have and the sometimes subtle threats they use. As long as it suits them it's acceptable. They manipulate the situation to shift the responsibility on to you.

If similar patterns begin to emerge in your relationship, then it might be timely to examine whether that relationship is right for you.

❀ Abusers use entitlement and threats to control your behaviour. These can be physical or emotional.

❀ Someone with a sense of entitlement will put themselves first and rarely consider your feelings. In a healthy relationship, partners care for each other equally.

✿ Abusers can use threats to get you to change your behaviour or become more like the person they want you to be, rather than letting you be who you are.

✿ Sometimes abusers threaten to hurt themselves or commit suicide if you won't do what they want. Talk to an adult or professional immediately if this happens to you.

CHAPTER 5

Psychological Abuse

Women in particular who have been abused tell me that psychological abuse is often the most difficult thing to deal with. They say that bruises, black eyes and broken bones heal, but it's the stuff that gets into your head that's the hardest to get over.

Although Sophie suffered two physical assaults by Weatherston before he killed her, they occurred well after their relationship had ended. During the five months they were seeing each other he was entirely psychologically abusive towards her; and that, it seems, is the most difficult to detect. Although it might seem callous, in some ways I now wish he had physically assaulted her early on. I've no doubt at all that Sophie would have been out of there fast.

From my work with the foundation, I've heard time and again that it's the slow build-up of abusive behaviour that's so confusing. Sophie didn't see the abuse coming and neither did I. If we — and I believe us both to be reasonably intelligent women — couldn't see the signs, then I surmise that there are many women, girls, men and boys who are similarly

unaware. That's why it is so important for me to see a
workshop like Loves-Me-Not come to fruition.

Name-calling

So what is psychological abuse? In Sophie's case, the
first and most obvious sign was name-calling. One
day Weatherston would say Sophie was beautiful and
another day he would say she was ugly. He called her fat,
ugly, stupid, slut and whore. When I read the Women's
Refuge website, those exact same words were listed
as common insults from abusers. Other sites about
domestic abuse use identical words. While I was doing
research for our educational awareness programme I
was corresponding with police in England. Among the
material they sent me was a story that appeared on the
BBC. This is what it said:

'A teenage girl, Taylah Douglas, spoke on the BBC
Newsnight programme. "When I first met him it was
good, he was my first proper boyfriend and it was kind of
like a movie," Taylah says of her boyfriend who she met
when they were both 16 years old. Within a short space
of time, still aged 16, she moved in with him and his
family. "He turned into a different person about two or
three months into the relationship," she says. "He would
call me fat and ugly and he would call me a slut." From
then on he would slap and punch Taylah and burn her
with lighters. She wasn't allowed to return home and he
confiscated her mobile phone. The assaults escalated.'

So there they are again — the same derogatory words. It almost seems as if there is a booklet — 'The A to Z of Being an Abuser'.

Sophie often used to say, 'He's doing my head in,' and I would think, he's doing mine in too, because I couldn't understand it. Psychological abuse usually consists of plenty of nasty statements and insults.

What troubled me most in Sophie's situation is that she actually believed what Weatherston said. I've heard it on many occasions over the past couple of years that the abused person believes what the abuser says about them. Sophie was no exception. She had a lovely figure and certainly wasn't fat — but she believed him. She would say, 'If I lost some weight off my behind he wouldn't say these things.' Now I might be biased, but I don't think my daughter was ugly. Weatherston would say things like her eyes were too close together or her ears stuck out. To me those were ridiculous statements, yet Sophie believed him. Again I'm told this is common in people suffering abuse — this belief in what's being said to them. I find that astonishing, but then I'm not in the position of being abused.

Sophie often used to say, 'He's doing my head in,' and I would think, he's doing mine in too, because I couldn't understand it. Psychological abuse usually consists of plenty of nasty statements and insults. To Sophie he could be extremely nice and flattering yet at other times he would say things like 'You are f***ing ugly and stupid and I never loved you anyway.' That kind of behaviour tends to make you feel bad about yourself. The result is often that the abused person blames themselves. You think you are not good enough, and that if you try harder to improve yourself you won't be treated like dirt.

Manipulation

I couldn't believe how fast Sophie's self-esteem plummeted. I guess it's understandable if you are going out with someone who says things like 'You are a f***ing horrible person that no one likes.' In some instances Weatherston quickly followed these put-downs with opposing comments such as 'You know how much I respect your intelligence and how good a friend I am.' I suppose if the put-downs were constant Sophie would have severed any ties to this man, but part of the manipulation was to turn on the charm while undermining her. Another day Sophie might be 'beautiful, bright and intelligent' and that 'we would go places'. It was never *you* would go places but always *we*. Then, depending on his mood, he might switch back to the derogatory remarks.

I recall at one stage, after things were relatively smooth, he suddenly said to Sophie, 'You are the most

Violence prevention through education, awareness and empowerment of young women.

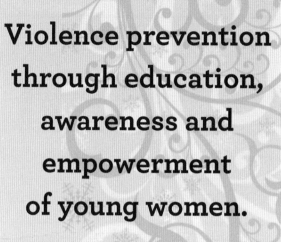

The Sophie Elliott Foundation logo styled on drawings Sophie sketched herself. Originally the foundation was concerned with educating and empowering young women, but is now equally concerned with educating young men as well.

POSITIVE RELATIONSHIP QUIZ

WHETHER YOU ARE IN A LONG-TERM OR CASUAL RELATIONSHIP, YOU DESERVE TO BE TREATED WELL AND ENSURE THAT YOU ARE TREATING YOUR PARTNER RESPECTFULLY.

TAKE THE QUIZ TO SEE HOW HEALTHY YOUR RELATIONSHIP IS. TICK YES OR NO.

	THE PERSON I AM WITH...	YES	NO
1.	Supports my choices	0	1
2.	Listens to my opinions	0	1
3.	Is positive and encourages me	0	1
4.	Accepts when I say I don't want to have sex	0	1
5.	Accepts what I wear and how I look	0	1
6.	Is not liked by my friends and family	1	0
7.	Makes me feel like I can't do anything right	1	0
8.	Makes fun of me or calls me names	1	0
9.	Sulks or gets angry when he/she doesn't get what they want	1	0
10.	Blames me for his/her problems	1	0
11.	Texts or calls me all the time to check up on me	5	0
12.	Makes it hard for me to see my friends and family and gets jealous when I do	5	0
13.	Pressures me to have sex or do things I don't want to	5	0
14.	Threatens to hurt himself/herself, me or others	5	0
15.	Does things that scare me (breaking things, yelling, driving fast)	5	0
	TOTAL	_____	

ABUSE AND CONTROLLING BEHAVIOURS ARE NEVER OK.

HELP IS AVAILABLE WHETHER YOU ARE BEING ABUSED OR BEING ABUSIVE. EVERYONE DESERVES TO BE TREATED WITH RESPECT.

IN A RELATIONSHIP, I...

		YES	NO
1.	Support my partner's decisions	0	1
2.	Get on OK with her/his friends and family	0	1
3.	Listen to her/his opinion	0	1
4.	Spend time by myself	0	1
5.	Trust my partner	0	1
6.	Criticise or make fun of her/him in front of others	1	0
7.	Get annoyed if I want sex but she/he doesn't	1	0
8.	Get jealous when she/he talks to others	1	0
9.	Constantly worry she/he is cheating on me	1	0
10.	Text or call all the time to check up on them	1	0
11.	Follow or check up on them (read their texts or emails)	5	0
12.	Often get upset about what she/he does	5	0
13.	Expect her/ him to tell me where they are all the time	5	0
14.	Think it's OK to be rough sometimes	5	0
15.	Take out my frustrations on her/him	5	0

TOTAL _____

SCORING

For questions 1-5
score one point for every NO

For questions 6-10
score one point for every YES

For questions 11-15
score five points for every YES

SCORE: 0 POINTS
Your relationship seems to be healthy and respectful.

SCORE: 1-2 POINTS
There may be a few unhealthy aspects to your relationship. This can be a warning sign that it will become more abusive. It's a good idea to address these early.

SCORE: 3-4 POINTS
There may be some warning signs that your relationship is abusive. It's important to take warning signs seriously as abuse can get worse over time.

SCORE: 5 POINTS OR MORE
There are definitely warning signs in your relationship. Abuse and controlling behaviours can get worse over time and it's sometimes hard to see how bad things have become.

IT IS OK TO ASK FOR HELP

If you are in danger call 111 and ask for Police

There are organisations in every community who can help. Find out what's available by phoning **0800 456 450** or visit **www.areyouok.org.nz**

POWER & CONTROL
in Dating Relationships

When one person in a relationship repeatedly scares, hurts
or puts down the other person, it is abuse.
The Power & Control Wheel lists examples of each form of abuse.
Remember, abuse is much more than slapping or grabbing someone.

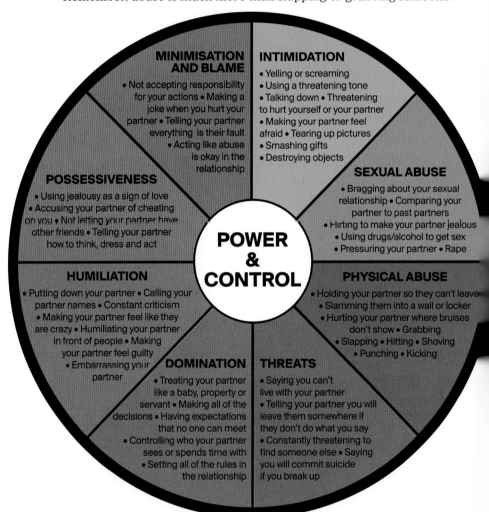

MINIMISATION AND BLAME
- Not accepting responsibility for your actions • Making a joke when you hurt your partner • Telling your partner everything is their fault • Acting like abuse is okay in the relationship

INTIMIDATION
- Yelling or screaming
- Using a threatening tone
- Talking down • Threatening to hurt yourself or your partner
- Making your partner feel afraid • Tearing up pictures
- Smashing gifts
- Destroying objects

POSSESSIVENESS
- Using jealousy as a sign of love
- Accusing your partner of cheating on you • Not letting your partner have other friends • Telling your partner how to think, dress and act

SEXUAL ABUSE
- Bragging about your sexual relationship • Comparing your partner to past partners
- Flirting to make your partner jealous
- Using drugs/alcohol to get sex
- Pressuring your partner • Rape

POWER & CONTROL

HUMILIATION
- Putting down your partner • Calling your partner names • Constant criticism
- Making your partner feel like they are crazy • Humiliating your partner in front of people • Making your partner feel guilty • Embarrassing your partner

PHYSICAL ABUSE
- Holding your partner so they can't leave
- Slamming them into a wall or locker
- Hurting your partner where bruises don't show • Grabbing
- Slapping • Hitting • Shoving
- Punching • Kicking

DOMINATION
- Treating your partner like a baby, property or servant • Making all of the decisions • Having expectations that no one can meet • Controlling who your partner sees or spends time with • Setting all of the rules in the relationship

THREATS
- Saying you can't live with your partner
- Telling your partner you will leave them somewhere if they don't do what you say
- Constantly threatening to find someone else • Saying you will commit suicide if you break up

A relationship full of control is really out of control.

Power & Control Wheel

Aged almost 16, Tania (not her real name) had been in
a relationship with a boy three years older than her.
Neither Tania's parents nor her friends approved of the
boyfriend, but Tania couldn't see past him. When he
bought her a phone and insisted on secrecy in much of
their relationship, she instinctively felt something was
not right. The relationship began to spiral out of her
control and ended in acrimony. Around this time, and
quite by chance, Tania saw a copy of the Power & Control
Wheel for dating relationships. It got her thinking about
the effects in her own situation. This is the list
of negative effects Tania wrote down:

- Encouraging me to lie and sneaking around behind
  my parents' backs.
- Continually bragging and comparing me to others.
- Using alcohol and drugs for sex.
- Applying pressures such as getting in the way of
  my friendships.
- In hindsight I felt used.
- To stop me telling the truth he threatened suicide.
- Blaming me for ruining his future.
- He made decisions for me.
- Controlling who I spent time with.
- Having fights over nothing — but it was always my fault.
- I ended up feeling guilty about lots of things.
- I wasn't allowed to talk to other boys.
- He was angry/violent/scary/shouting.
- Broke his hand punching a wall in front of others.
- Not accepting responsibility for himself.
- Accusing me and talking down to me.
- Making me feel afraid.
- Destroying things of mine.
- Smashing a beer bottle near me when he was drunk.

All of these things had a negative impact on
Tania's relationship.

- Does it sound familiar?
- Would the idea of recording your experiences help?

Right Sophie and me. She could share anything with me and I urge young people to have a special person you can confide in.

Below Sophie and Kade. She adored him and soon after Sophie died, so did Kade.

Left Clara, Jess and Sophie.

Below Kate, Sophie and Clara. Great friends. When a partner begins to alienate you from close or long-time friendships regard this as a big warning sign.

Above Sophie
achieved well
academically but
she worked hard
for her success.

Sophie Kate Elliott
(11.6.1985 to 9.1.2008)

selfish person ever. I hate you half the time. There are a lot of things I don't like about you.' This to me is very odd behaviour.

Sophie's moods reflected his treatment of her. She would come in the door and I'd call out 'How was your day?' Often she would come in smiling and bubbly, but some days there would be silence. Increasingly she would come home and burst into tears. This, from what I have learned since Sophie died, is quite common among abused women. They go downhill — fast.

If a partner wants you to change that much, perhaps you should be asking yourself if your relationship is equal, or whether it's rapidly becoming a controlling one?

The most disturbing aspect from my point of view is the degree to which the abused person takes the blame for the abuser's behaviour, by feeling bad about themselves. They think that if they were better people they wouldn't bring on the abuse. I would have thought that if anyone was attracted to you then it's for who and what you are. Why should you have to change your lifestyle, looks and behaviours to suit him or her? If a partner wants you to change that much, perhaps you should be asking yourself if your relationship is equal, or whether it's rapidly becoming a controlling one?

Manipulative behaviour is certainly a sign to be aware of and it comes in many guises. In Sophie's case it usually revolved around Weatherston's selfish demands. As I've said in Chapter 3, there was sometimes little or no contact between them all week then he would phone to say he wanted to go out. His expectation was that Sophie should drop everything, even if she had an assignment due, to please him. She might have been reluctant to go but didn't want to disappoint him so did as he asked. There must be something quite powerful at work in a controlling relationship because Sophie had a strong character and could certainly stand up for herself. Yet strangely she put up with his demands or expectations in a way I can't comprehend.

Self-centredness

Occasionally Weatherston would be late for dates or not be at the place they had arranged to meet. When he did answer his mobile phone or reply to a text he'd have some feeble excuse about meeting someone, forgetting the time, was late from the gym, or some other reason. There was always an excuse but never an apology. If Sophie did get cross with him or complain he'd accuse her of not caring about him.

Similarly this 'it's all about me' attitude continued in their social life. Sophie was never invited to go out with his friends, but he expected to come along to anything involving hers. And as I've mentioned, Sophie was always the sober driver. On more than

one occasion she said to me, 'You know, just for once I
wish he'd be the sober driver so I could have a drink.'
But he never did.

Weatherston knew that Sophie loved to dance.
She'd been a dancer all her life and started ballet
lessons at age four. Out socially, he would often ignore
her and dance with others or even by himself. He was,
by all accounts, a flamboyant person, but on the dance
floor it was more about a performance than sharing an
enjoyable moment. Often this flamboyance (or showing
off) could be quite embarrassing. The following excerpt
from *Sophie's Legacy* illustrates the point:

Another sign of his unusual behaviour came
about on 14 September 2007. The university
PhD ball was being held at Larnach Castle.
He came to our home to pick up Sophie and
I must admit they both looked nice. I took
a photo of them but had to encourage them
to put their arms around each other, which
he did somewhat reluctantly. Sophie told
me how he would become quite attentive
if it seemed there was someone to impress,
but more ambivalent when they were alone.
Where Sophie was very complimentary
about the way he looked he was far more
reserved and made what I would describe as
nothing more than a passing comment on
her appearance. All of these sorts of things
are really of little consequence on their own
but collectively tend to show how everything

had to revolve around him. The day after
the ball Sophie said it went well although
embarrassing as Clayton's self-centred
personality was on display for all to see. On
arriving at the castle he noticed there were
a couple of seats vacant beside the vice
chancellor and he made a beeline for them
and, uninvited, took that prime position. He
regularly made an exhibition of himself on
the dance floor and generally made it clear
people should notice him.

I've mentioned this and other incidents not to demonise
Weatherston, but to illustrate how self-centredness is
a trait of a psychological abuser. They want their
partner to be subservient to them — in other words to
be worthless, which in their mind means 'worth less
than me'.

❀ Psychological abuse can be the
hardest to get over because it can
undermine your sense of self-worth.
Abused people end up believing what
their abuser is telling them, even if
it's not true.
❀ Name-calling is psychological abuse,
and can happen early on in a relationship.
❀ Manipulating someone's emotions
is also psychological abuse. This

could be making negative remarks
followed up by positive ones, so
you're never sure what that person
really thinks about you.

✿ People who are psychologically
abused begin to take the blame for
the abuser's behaviour on themselves.
Remember, no one person is to blame
for all the problems in a relationship.

✿ If your moods have changed
dramatically and your self-esteem
is low since being in a particular
relationship it could be an unhealthy
relationship.

✿ Self-centredness is a trait of
a psychological abuser. If you
challenge this behaviour they may
use manipulation to say that you
don't care enough for them.

CHAPTER 6

Physical Abuse

Clayton Weatherston never physically assaulted Sophie until 10 days before she died and by that time the relationship was already over. Sure, there had been plenty of psychological abuse, including him shouting and yelling at her, but never a physical assault.

Never been so scared in all her life

Soon after Sophie finally ended her relationship with Weatherston and had completed her final examinations, she went to Australia for a holiday. The previous months of study coupled with an on-again, off-again confusing relationship had taken its toll. Her moods were less even and accompanied by floods of tears, which was most un-Sophie-like. Sophie and her best friend went to Melbourne and Sydney to visit Sophie's two brothers then headed off for some sightseeing in Queensland. When Sophie got home she looked a million dollars, all ready to take on the next stage of her life.

She went into full-time work at a photographic shop until it was time to leave for Wellington and her first career opportunity as a graduate analyst at Treasury. Photography had been Sophie's passion for years and, Sophie being Sophie, she offered to take photographs of Weatherston's graduation that December. Sophie never wanted to end with anyone on a bad note, and said she would be happy to record Weatherston's big day — despite the relationship being over. He accepted this gesture. She took photographs of his PhD graduation and the social event that followed at a Dunedin restaurant. There were the usual photos of him wearing his regalia and less formal ones of his family trying the regalia on. All in all they were very good photographs.

Sophie had the pictures developed and put together a nice album. She came to me after Christmas and said she wanted to give him the album, but didn't know how. I thought that his odd behaviour during their relationship was such that he didn't, in my opinion, deserve much consideration. I suggested she either take it to the university and flick it under his door or post it to him. However, Sophie wanted to personally hand him the album. I think she wanted to see his reaction. Perhaps she was proud of the way she had presented a pictorial record of a special day. Sophie sent him a text to say she had something for him and could she bring it over to his flat. Sophie told me that on arriving at his flat he had a cursory glance at the album, said it was nice and casually dropped it on the floor. He said he wanted to go to bed with her, but she firmly rejected his advances. The relationship was well over; she was heading to Wellington in less than a fortnight and would probably never see him again. He then picked her up and threw her onto his bed. He put one arm across her throat and a hand over her mouth, all the time shouting obscenities at her.

Sophie was about five foot four and weighed 50 kilograms, whereas he was over six feet tall and 92 kilograms, so physically she didn't have a chance. I asked Sophie how she escaped and she said they were struggling so much they fell from the bed and she managed to run from his flat out to her car. He followed, screaming abuse at her. Sophie told me later she had never been so scared in all her life.

She was shaking so much that rather than risk driving home she went to her workplace which was nearby. Her friends calmed her down with a coffee and comforting words. They urged Sophie to go to the police and report the assault, but she didn't take up the suggestion. She said she had thought about it, but what was the point? It would basically be her word against his and it would all become a big hassle she could do without. She had no physical injuries to show for the ordeal, and as she was about to shift away she would never see him again and wanted to just forget it.

When Sophie came home and told me what had happened I was mortified. I couldn't believe someone could do this to my daughter. I know a lot of people suffering partner abuse get more than what he dished out to Sophie, but that doesn't minimise what he did. I couldn't understand it. He hadn't been physically abusive before. Like Sophie's workmates, I urged her to go to the police station. I offered to go with her, but again she rationalised the futility of reporting the incident. She was about to leave town and just wanted to put it behind her.

And guess what? I agreed with her. Ten days later she was dead.

To illustrate what Sophie was up against, I want to share an anecdote. When I was writing *Sophie's Legacy* I came upon a taxi driver who had seen Weatherston's 'wilder' side and I can now understand why Sophie would have been so terrified. Here is the taxi driver's account of what she saw, an account that shows how irrational that man could be:

*It was on a very wet night in November 2007.
I received a call to pick up a passenger from
the student area by the name of Sophie. As
I arrived this young woman came running
along the path closely followed by a clearly
angry man. He was making gestures with
his hands and obviously threatening.
Sophie jumped into the cab and closed the
door. The man leaned over the front of my
car with his face close to the windscreen.
I've been driving taxis for a long time and
have seen all sorts of people, some nice*

*and some nasty. This fellow was definitely
creepy and sent a shiver down my spine.
He wasn't shouting or anything like that
which probably made me feel even more
uncomfortable, but he was very frightening.
During the incident this fellow was so
focused on Sophie that he seemed unaware
of my presence, but I won't forget the look
in his eyes. Sophie was shaking and quite
terrified at this outburst and I wasted no
time in leaving.*

*I said to Sophie, 'Don't tell me that guy is
your boyfriend.' She said he was an ex. We
got talking, as cabbies and passengers do,
and Sophie told me about him and some
of his controlling habits like checking her
mobile for texts and phone calls. She was
a bubbly little thing with a great smile, and
although she seemed to relax it was obvious
she had been quite terrified. This incident
was so significantly different to most other
incidents that I even mentioned it to family
members the next day.*

*When I saw Weatherston's photo in the
newspaper after Sophie's murder I knew,
without any doubt whatsoever, that he was
the crazy man I'd seen threatening Sophie.*

I implore people who are in physically abusive
relationships to not accept this type of behaviour. Say

no to abuse. If it happens, even once, report it to the police. By not doing so we are simply condoning the behaviour; if we accept abuse we can never hope to come to terms with it.

Stay away

Two days before Sophie died she went down to the university with a gift for her supervisor. He wasn't in so she left the gift on his desk. Unfortunately Weatherston was there, saw Sophie and said, 'Come down to my office — we need to talk.' Regrettably she did go into his office and he closed the door. He wrapped his arms around her but she was shaking as the recent assault was still in her mind. He asked her why she was shaking and she said, 'Because of what you did to me the other day.' He pushed her back and said, 'And what was that?' Sophie told me later that she just lost it. She said she put one arm across his throat and her hand over his mouth and yelled, 'This is what you did to me. It's assault and my friends and my mum say I can go to the police.' Weatherston simply said, 'Well, you've assaulted me now and I can go to the police.'

So Sophie wasn't going to win. She ran from his office along to a stairwell, but he followed and shoved her hard. She said by the grace of God she managed to hang on to a railing and didn't fall. She asked Weatherston why he pushed her and he replied, 'I'm giving you my hate.'

When Sophie told me what happened I said, 'Soph, you've just got to keep away from him.'

In January there aren't usually many people in tertiary institutions, however he was there and so too were a number of others. After Sophie died, the police investigation revealed that several people heard the commotion between Weatherston and Sophie yet not one person thought to intervene. I often wonder if things might have turned out differently if just one of them had left their office and said, 'Hey guys, what's going on?' This is called the bystander effect and I'll talk about this later in the chapter.

Patterns of behaviour

Another revelation came about during the investigation. We found out from police that Sophie wasn't the only woman who Weatherston had either physically or psychologically abused or who had felt threatened in his presence. For one reason or another they had managed to get away from him. Either their studies finished and they were leaving the university or, like Sophie, they were shifting away from Dunedin. Not one of those women reported an assault, but then neither did Sophie.

From bitter experience I can say that every instance of assault should be reported. It may not end in a prosecution but at least it might show concerning behaviour. Police have developed a system where instances of abuse are recorded. There may not be sufficient evidence or other reason to go through to a prosecution, but the records could show a pattern of behaviour. Even if each of the women involved with Weatherston had reported his behaviour none of it may have ended up in an arrest (although one ex-girlfriend called to give evidence at Weatherston's trial had a story to tell that would almost certainly have seen him before the courts). However, what it would have done is show his pattern of behaviour. Then, if Sophie had reported her attacks police would have been able to establish that this was regularly happening, thus taking her complaint more seriously than she expected them to.

So my advice to anyone who is physically abused is to report it to the police. Such behaviour has to stop and the only way we can do this is to have absolute zero tolerance to abuse.

Don't be a bystander

The bystander effect is something that causes me concern. I've done quite a bit of research about this phenomenon and it's a very real issue. Too often we hear of some terrible tragedy unfolding, only to then listen to bystanders, such as family or neighbours, saying, 'I thought something bad was happening there but didn't want to get involved.' For years, relationship violence was something others didn't want to acknowledge. If you can't intervene or you feel unsafe, at least tell someone. Police, in particular, have trained staff who can sort out these problems. I know it's not easy interfering in the lives of others, but left unchecked a violent relationship will only escalate.

Take, for instance, Emily Longley. In England in 2011, Emily, a New Zealander, died at the hands of a boyfriend she was trying to get away from. He told several people he was going to kill her, yet no one intervened. No one took his threats seriously. I say get involved. If it turns out to be someone letting off steam, so be it. My view is that it's better to be safe than sorry.

Abuse doesn't always end in tragic circumstances, as it did for Sophie and Emily, but why should any young person have to suffer any sort of fear or torment from the person who is supposed to love them?

I can imagine a situation where a young man says to his friend, 'Hey, mate, I don't like the way you're treating your girlfriend.' The response will probably be, 'Butt out, mate, it's none of your damned business.' I say make it your business. Keep people accountable. We can all do something by taking a zero tolerance approach to abuse.

Keep safe

In summary, I ask you: In your relationship, do differences of opinion or arguments lead to hitting, punching or strangling? If they do, my advice is to end the relationship. No one deserves that sort of treatment.

From what I understand now, strangling is a particularly important warning sign. Police tell me that when a woman reports abuse they usually look at her neck first to see if there are finger-size bruises. Strangling is quite common in physically abusive relationships. When Weatherston attacked Sophie the first time he applied pressure to her throat.

Relationships end for all sorts of reasons and most people get over them. I want to stress that what happened to Sophie was at the extreme end. Break-ups and rejections can lead to anger and hurt feelings that at times lead to quite volatile situations. These situations should be taken seriously, and if in doubt seek help early on. I reiterate my advice to anyone in a relationship that turns violent, or if your partner threatens to physically abuse you — walk away and report the incident.

❀ Avoid contact with your abuser. Their behaviour will usually get worse, not better.

❀ Physical violence can escalate quickly. There were only 10 days between Weatherston's first physical attack on Sophie and her death.

❀ A partner who physically abuses you may have a history of abusing

others. Report any incidents to
the police so they can establish a
pattern of behaviour.

❀ The whole community has to
have an attitude of zero tolerance
towards physical abuse. Don't stand
by if you think someone you know
is being abused.

❀ When a relationship breaks up this
can potentially be a dangerous
time, especially if your partner is
angry. If you are worried about an
angry response, seek advice from
an agency beforehand.

❀ Avoid breaking up by text or on
Facebook.

❀ If you are the person feeling angry or
hurt, talk it over with someone rather
than getting into a confrontation you
might later regret.

CHAPTER 7

Sexual Abuse

There were issues in Sophie's relationship with Clayton Weatherston that fall under the heading of sexual abuse. For reasons of decency and out of respect for Sophie's dignity I don't intend going into these in detail. However, sexual issues will quite possibly play a part in an unhealthy relationship.

When I talk of sexual abuse I'm mainly referring to things like unwanted touching or when you are forced to have sex when you don't want to. Such behaviour is rape or sexual assault and on the statute books that is a very serious crime. If anyone is forcing you to have sex they are committing a crime. Likewise someone taking advantage of you because you're drunk is not okay. Like physical abuse, you need to report this. Less serious but still destructive is when one partner continually pesters the other to have sex, even though they may not want to.

In the case of girls in particular, if a boy's pressuring

you for sex after one or two dates, do you think that is safe? At age 13 or 14 it is probably dangerous, quite apart from it being against the law. Girls this age are seldom emotionally mature enough to handle the 'bonding' to an inappropriate boy once sexual activity starts. Of course it is confusing if others start calling you a prude or saying that 'Everyone's doing it — what's wrong with you?' If you are not emotionally prepared for a sexual relationship then difficulties arise. Perhaps ask yourself, 'Am I prepared to put up with this pressure of him wanting sex?' If it doesn't feel right then it probably isn't.

One thing I can say about Sophie's relationship with Weatherston is that his issues were turned around so that Sophie would take the blame for any problems — in other words, she would think, 'If I were a better person this wouldn't happen.'

The following is from *Sophie's Legacy*:

> *Sexual issues were where Clayton Weatherston's narcissistic personality really came to the fore. Sophie told me that she felt Clayton was insecure in that he needed constant reinforcement about how good he was in all sorts of ways. She said he never offered her any support; it was always one-sided. I don't think she had struck this kind of personality before and it caused her further confusion and anxiety. He made Sophie feel as if his inadequacies were her fault. Sophie confided in me on even more*

*intimate matters. She told me one of his
annoying habits was to continually want
her to draw comparisons between him and
any of her previous partners. Although
she was reluctant to get drawn into these
psychological games, she said he just went
on and on about it — was he as good as,
or better than other men, sort of thing. I
became aware of one occasion where Sophie
finally relented and told him. Clayton was
not pleased and she regretted having said
anything. She told me he was very persistent
when it came to sexual issues and wouldn't
accept no for an answer. I don't know if
Sophie really knew how to respond to this.*

*I know Sophie worked hard, often
under stress, but I never thought it would
necessitate her wanting to see a counsellor.
So when she asked me what she should
do, it came as quite a shock. Although I
didn't appreciate it at the time, it is quite
appropriate for students of Sophie's age
to seek counselling when faced with
relationship breakdowns. Personally I
think what compounded Sophie's normally
stressful times with study, work, socialising
and everything that goes with it was this sort
of weird on-again off-again relationship, his
meanness and self-centred attitude and what
I consider his obsession with sex. Sophie took
this personally and by implication thought*

any sexual problems exhibited by him were
her fault, that she wasn't 'sexy' enough
for him. That, coupled with him in one
breath saying she was beautiful and would
go places, then in the next saying she was
ugly, fat and useless, helped lower her self-
esteem greatly. It still angers but at the same
time perplexes me as to why she kept going
back to him. He must have had something
in his make-up that kept attracting her
— a sort of persuasiveness, I guess. It was
only later, after having sought an in-depth
understanding of narcissism, that I came
to grips with what that hold really entails.
And it is a powerful hold.

If your partner is making you feel that you're not 'hot'
enough for them, or is blaming you for any of their
inadequacies, then it is not an equal relationship.

Staying healthy

In an equal relationship you should both take responsibility for contraception, no matter which method
you decide to use. Your partner refusing to use
contraception, of any kind or to discuss it with you is
a sign of an unhealthy relationship. When it comes to
the question of contraception one might ask, 'Whose
responsibility is it?' I say clearly to girls, 'If it's not a

joint decision then make it your responsibility.' If not you can end up carrying the baby — literally. Or you might end up with a sexually transmitted disease. If you're not sure of the options you can go to a Family Planning clinic for advice about avoiding pregnancy or STDs.

Pornography

I want to touch on the issue of pornography. Your partner may demand that you watch pornography when you're not comfortable doing so. I'm not so naïve to think it's not readily available; I know the internet has made it more accessible. However, from research I have read and from speaking with professionals working in the area of abuse, viewing and downloading pornography are habits of a classic abuser.

It should therefore have come as no surprise to me that, following an audit by the university, Weatherston was found to have been downloading porn late at night in his office. I would have thought that someone of his supposed intellect wouldn't have done it at work. Perhaps he thought he wouldn't be caught. An occasional look at a site is one thing, but I've been assured his usage was hours and hours on end.

So my advice in this regard is simple: if a partner spends a lot of time accessing or downloading porn and insisting you watch it when you don't want to, alarm bells should begin to ring — listen to them.

❀ Pressuring someone for sex or using threats to get sex are signs of an unhealthy relationship.

❀ If you are having sex, you and your partner should discuss what kind of contraception you want to use. If your partner says it's your problem, that's not sharing the responsibility equally.

❀ A partner blaming you for their inadequacies is not healthy.

❀ If your partner spends a lot of time watching pornography and insists you watch it when you don't want to, that is not part of a healthy relationship.

CHAPTER 8

Navigating Love

By Gayna McConnell

Navigating the wonderfully twisty world of new love is complex enough without finding ourselves with a person who either doesn't know how to love, or even worse, actually wants to hurt us. How can this happen? How can normal, intelligent people end up in the sticky web of unhealthy love? Or end up with a partner who is selfish and controlling? There are so many reasons young people get lost in relationships. Mostly it comes down to us not being prepared for the possible traps and realities that get in the way of 'happily ever after'.

While some people are incapable of unconditionally loving another human being, the majority of us can learn what healthy love and caring is all about. Trusting our own lovability, communicating who we are and learning to handle our emotions under stress opens up the potential for a great relationship. It also enables us to get away from a bad one.

Some young people report being abused by a partner. Clayton Weatherston was at the extreme end of a continuum. Most young people will probably experience the confusion of being involved in varying degrees of unhealthy love at some stage, especially as they enter longer-term relationships, or when they look back on old ones. Lesley Elliott has detailed clearly what to look out for in people who are unhealthy partners. This chapter focuses on the forces at play in the current climate of finding love and the reasons people may justify, minimise and ignore the sometimes neon-lit signs of potentially abusive partners.

There are old and new realities that come together as you enter a relationship with someone else. Some of you may have been involved in committed relationships for years; others may have only had a few forays into flirting, or something in between. Either way, you have probably felt how your gender influences you in a way that it doesn't in friendships. Relationships bring downloaded messages about fairy-tale love and acting in certain ways to fit in with our peers. The majority of us unwittingly play out these messages that are reinforced in music, videos, television and movies. These mixed messages are about sexiness, power and superficial versions of love.

The expansive realms of cyberspace

We are not taught much about what to expect in terms of the feelings and pressures that may come up when we enter a relationship. Many young people start their relationships in the expansive realms of cyberspace, which is often fraught with difficulty. Here we have an arena where fantasy rules and true colours can be 'photoshopped' and 'filtered'. This also adds to the potential for messy first likes, lusts and loves. Parents and adults are generally naïve to the realities of what adolescents are doing, saying and seeing online. The hidden nature of online socialising means young people have to navigate these new horizons alone, and are often ill-prepared for the complexities and confusions that will undoubtedly arise.

Most adults don't know that from the age of 13 or 14 it's not uncommon to have a thousand Facebook 'friends', or be entrenched in the anonymous questioning site Ask.fm. They probably don't know how accessible Snapchat is, or that you possibly have thousands of Twitter followers. They will also not be aware of various hook-up sites and apps such as

Tinder. These sites will in all probability be replaced by others quite rapidly, but the dangers will be ever present. These social domains and mobile phones not only plug you into cyberspace, but also into the pockets of hundreds of other people. They also open up the world of intimate relationships in ways most adults couldn't even imagine.

When it comes to relationships, Facebook is a common medium for starting one, but when a young person 'private messages' someone, the conversation often becomes sexually suggestive very quickly. What's being communicated, and the possible expectations that come with it, have the potential to set young people up in situations they are not prepared for, with people they don't really know. The adults in their world are often completely unaware, and generally young people will go to lengths to keep it that way.

Interest and access to the social media world is not going to lessen, so being aware of the dynamics that this world brings to relationships is important. Facebook especially opens up the 'dating game' for everyone. If someone wants a relationship, or something more casual, social media offers a smorgasbord of opportunities for lust and love. But it also brings superficial pressures of perfection and competition that raise insecurities of 'not being good enough'. People who are engaging manipulators, such as Weatherston, target these insecurities with charm and flattering words, while manipulative behaviours, such as put-downs and guilt trips, are eagerly waiting in the wings.

Anticipation and expectations

New relationships can bring up feelings of excitement about potential sex, and being wanted or desired. These feelings pump up 'feel good' hormones and are mostly based on anticipation and fantasy mixed in with romantic ideals and peer pressure. This can create difficulties. Being influenced by gender stereotypes and limiting beliefs regarding our self-worth can hamper our ability to really know what we want. This in turn can limit our ability to speak up for it. If messages, pressures and dynamics are not neutralised by being understood for what they really are, what happens? It becomes a challenge to communicate and behave in a way that is in line with who we really are.

In any new relationship there are always unspoken expectations, assumptions and power dynamics to negotiate. In knowing this, we can be more prepared and willing to communicate clearly. When we do, we give potential partners the opportunity to show us who they are by allowing them to either hear our points of view or respectfully respond to us. This is a good starting point to see if there is potential for a healthy relationship to take place.

A lot can still get in the way, especially for newbies to relationships, of being able to openly communicate thoughts, feelings, and needs. That's because most of us are not taught how to be good communicators.

This is particularly so when we feel anxious or under stress. Why? Because it is within intimate relationships that our hidden insecurities about our 'okay-ness' come to the surface. Added to that is our culture of predominately non-verbal communication. Alcohol and drugs, along with gender norms of being polite and/or horny, also have a part to play.

When chatting via social media, think about:

WHAT DO I WANT?

WHAT DOES THE OTHER PERSON WANT?

AM I INVOLVED WITH CHAT ETC. THAT EXPRESSES WHO I AM?

AM I SETTING UP EXPECTATIONS AND AN IMAGE OF MYSELF THAT IS NOT IN LINE WITH WHO I REALLY AM?

Power imbalances

Regarding relationships, gender has us acting like we are still in the 1980s. From what I hear from young people, there are often power imbalances right at the start of relationships. Power is often given, not taken, away. It seems adolescent females are especially vulnerable to being self-sacrificing and submissive to a partner's needs in order to maintain their interest. When a potential partner says to her that she is hot and beautiful, these words can be powerful. They probably make her feel special, wanted and excited at a time when other relationships in her life may be giving her messages she is not okay. If that partner starts to remove their attention she may begin to feel worthless and unlovable because she has based her worth on the other person's attention and opinion.

Females might be more vulnerable to being hurt by partner violence, but either sex can find themselves in a relationship where their partner holds the other person responsible for their emotional state. Unhealthy partners do this using guilt trips, manipulation and threats to get their own way and maintain a sense of power. As Lesley has said, this behaviour may start subtly, but over time becomes the dominant trait of an unhealthy partner.

Putting yourself second, or worrying about 'hurting someone's feelings' can leave you open to being taken advantage of. Lesley said this about Sophie too — that she was 'above all, caring, pleased people before herself, and was too forgiving of the way Weatherston treated and spoke to her'. Isn't your happiness the most important thing? Sacrificing your own voice and happiness to keep your partner happy is actually a sign of a lack of self-respect. This is one of the key elements that enables patterns of put-downs and abusive behaviour to develop.

IT TAKES TIME TO REALLY KNOW SOMEONE, BUT ONCE THEY SHOW YOU — TRUST THAT.

Healthy relationships come from healthy people who bring together a combination of chemistry, self-respect, empathy and brave communication. It's important not to sacrifice your self-respect in relationships. Self-respect is tied to accepting yourself, and the majority of us are not very good at doing that. If you don't really like and accept yourself, you will struggle trusting that someone else likes and accepts you. This doubt can set up a breeding ground for insecurities, letting unhealthy power and control dynamics sneak in. As in Sophie's relationship, an unhealthy partner will get into your head and play on your own fears and insecurities for their own gain.

> # PARTNERS MAY NOT ALWAYS BE ABLE TO BUILD YOU UP, BUT IT'S DANGEROUS GROUND WHEN THEY TRY TO BRING YOU DOWN.

Being assertive in the face of manipulative or confusing behaviour may be uncomfortable and create conflict. However, this is an essential part of negotiating relationships. Speaking up about what you will and won't put up with is often enough for a reasonably healthy person to rein in their behaviour. If they don't, they are showing their true colours. The true colours of an obviously unhealthy person will likely get worse. Pay attention to the warning signs Lesley talked about, because there is a certain percentage of unhealthy people who are wired in a way most of us will never understand. You, or someone you care about, may need help and support to get out of a relationship if they are caught up in one like that.

Relationship boundaries

Relationship boundaries are the rules and limits we set for ourselves about how we expect to be treated and the behaviours we deem okay. We know when someone is pushing against our boundaries by the way we feel about something they said or how they behaved. When someone leaves us feeling annoyed, uncomfortable, or with other negative emotions, then they have come up against one of our boundaries.

❀ Take time to think about why you feel the way you do.

❀ Think about your feelings and thoughts and what they tell you about yourself.

❀ What do your thoughts and feelings tell you about the other person?

❀ Where possible, bring up your feelings and concerns with your partner when you are calm, because when people communicate from a place of anger or hurt, they often come across as attacking and blaming. This can trigger the other person to attack and blame back.

We all desire relationships that are fun and respectful. However, not all potential partners will be right for us and it is up to us to be on the ball when the behaviour of someone else makes us feel unhappy. Negative behaviours in relationships are often hidden behind initial flattery and charm — like Lesley said: 'Part of the manipulation is to turn on the charm.' Know and expect that the first few weeks of a relationship is usually a period of best behaviour and excitement. And also remember that it takes time to get to know someone. In a way we are teaching others how to treat us by what we are prepared to put up with, and whether or not we speak up if they come against our boundaries.

It is common to enter the dating world with weak boundaries, because of how we think we are meant to love and because we are not taught about the importance of strong boundaries. Without them we end up confused about where we stop and the other person begins. This happens because we give our power away when we make others responsible for the good and the bad feelings we have about ourselves. The way to strengthen our boundaries is by being responsible for ourselves and deciding how we let others affect us. When the moment arises, and it will when another's behaviour comes up against your boundaries, this is the time to speak up.

Unhealthy partners initially push boundaries to get their own way by using emotional tactics such as guilt, fear and shame; by getting moody or sulky; or by yelling and using put-downs. They may be jealous and possessive, and they will also attempt to make others change plans in order to suit them. With very unhealthy partners, these manipulative behaviours escalate over time and become mixed with attempts to isolate you from your friends and family by controlling you. This is usually characterised by using threats, disrespect, emotional blackmail and violence.

Unhealthy male or female partners can also resort to threats of self-harm or suicide to manipulate and control their partners, especially if their partner is trying to end the relationship. As Lesley said, this behaviour is hard to navigate at any age, especially if the partner attempts to follow through with the threat. But always know that the threat of suicide should never be a tool used to hold you in a relationship that you are desperate to get out of. Always help yourself, and anyone else in this type of relationship, to get all the help needed to break free.

Right from the beginning of a relationship it is our responsibility to repeatedly give our partners the message that they are the only ones responsible for their behaviour. If your partner blames you for 'making them' act in a certain way, know within yourself that they alone are responsible for controlling their behaviour. If you find yourself with someone who continues to hold you accountable for their feelings, such as insecurities, jealousy or anger, it is your job to speak up, and if nothing changes, to get out.

Most of us give strong non-verbal messages about what we do and don't like, but clear verbal communication is vital for letting others know your boundaries. The earlier you assert your boundaries

within new relationships, the earlier you will know if
this person is safe for you or not.

> SO PRACTISE SPEAKING UP; PRACTISE
> COMMUNICATING CLEARLY WHAT
> YOU THINK AND FEEL BY USING
> 'I' STATEMENTS. SAY NO FIRMLY,
> AND YES CLEARLY. AND ABOVE ALL,
> SPEAK UP FOR YOUR OWN NEEDS IF
> YOU ARE BEING TREATED IN A WAY
> THAT DOESN'T SIT RIGHT WITH YOU.

If others treat us badly it can come as a shock, or we
can take some time to notice it. Either way, it is often
confusing and mixed in with our caring for them. Over
time, others' actions always show us who they are.
Allow time to really get to know someone and focus
on their actions. This will show you who they are, and
whether they really care about you.

Lost in love

People with a low belief in their own worth are vulnerable to losing themselves in the rush of a new relationship. This is because they can give away their power by unconsciously relying on the other person to help them feel whole. A relationship like this can, for both parties, feel quite intoxicating and intense at first. But as time goes by it can become confusing and stifling as each person struggles to maintain their own sense of identity and personal power. Someone who gives their power away may get to a point where they believe they can't live without their partner. This only increases those insecurities which in turn often makes their partner pull further away. It becomes easy to end up feeling trapped in this type of unhealthy relationship because the foundations of it are based on control and neediness rather than love and respect.

Time is needed to truly know if a relationship has the potential to be nurturing or neurotic. So hold yourself back. Practise speaking up for your needs and boundaries and give the other person time to show you who they really are. It takes about three months for someone to show their true colours — up until then the majority of people are on their best behaviour. For most, the first month or so is pretty good, with lots of anticipation, firsts and fantasy. Even though unhealthy relationships emerge subtly to become more and more obvious as time goes by, people caught up in them almost always say there were warning bells that they minimised or ignored. Often these warning bells are there from early on in the relationship. In Sophie's case, they were obvious within three weeks.

In an unhealthy relationship the other person will try to control and seize power by saying and doing things to make you feel small and inadequate. They may also be irrational and heap blame on you. These put-downs and guilt trips are commonly disguised as 'jokes', when in reality they belittle you. If you are having a good laugh at the name-calling, then that is one thing. However, if underneath you feel bad, annoyed or hurt by something your partner said or insinuated, then you need to speak up about it. As happened to Sophie, this type of behaviour can quickly erode someone's sense of self and lower their self-esteem.

It is not easy speak up and challenge how someone treats you. When you are aware that someone has pushed against your boundaries and you experience negative feelings you have two options: either speak up or do nothing. By doing nothing you give the message that 'how you treated me was okay', and more than likely the person will repeat and escalate the behaviour. By immediately speaking up you have a chance to nip the behaviour in the bud, or find out if they are a healthy, safe person for you or not. It is your job to reinforce the message that you won't accept being put down, controlled or manipulated — and mean what you say. For instance you could say:

> 'I WAS CONFUSED WHEN YOU SPOKE TO ME COLDLY LAST NIGHT. I DIDN'T THINK IT WAS FAIR.'

Extremely unhealthy people like Clayton Weatherston will never change. They will get aggressive, blaming or manipulative, then switch their behaviour to charming to keep the upper hand in the relationship. If you find yourself caught up with someone who has this type of personality, it will not get better. Get all the help you need to get out.

Shields of protection

Feeling resilient and strong 100 per cent of the time is pretty tough. Not only may we find ourselves involved in challenging intimate relationships, but friendships, online interactions and relationships at home can also be hostile and unsupportive. This can batter our self-confidence. A concept that can help us avoid getting lost in other people's emotional baggage is that of a 'shield'. It enables us to deflect comments so that we are not so easily affected by emotions such as hurt and anger.

> USE THE VISUAL IMAGE OF WORDS BEING OBJECTS THAT OTHERS THROW AT YOU. NOW IMAGINE A SHIELD DEFLECTING THEM — STOPPING LETTING THEM IN TO UPSET OR HURT YOU.

This can help you avoid a flight or fight response and remain calm and assertive. The behaviour can then be addressed calmly and in a more 'hearable' way. Shields are a way of bringing resilience (strength) into your life and enable you to see that other people's words can't really hurt you. Rather, they can show you clearly who that person really is.

Another way to protect yourself is to imagine that the person using abusive words is speaking a different language. You don't understand the language, so the words can't hurt you. Again, see past attempts to make you feel small and see the true colours of the person speaking the words.

An abusive person is always driven by their own fears and insecurities, and this is what motivates them to prevent their partners being themselves. When we have a clear sense of who we are, we are less likely to feel threatened or unsafe by relying on a partner. Ideally we should be able to appreciate and enjoy the qualities in a partner that make them unique, rather than trying to manipulate, control or change them. Relationships are challenging and it is not always smooth sailing, but with self-acceptance and an acceptance of our partners, relationships can provide a safe space in which we can grow and be supported.

A healthy relationship has all the elements of a good friendship and includes varying degrees of physicality. It is when two people enjoy spending time together, are involved in a balanced way in each other's life and are respected and cared for by each other. Boundaries, communication, honesty and trust are essential foundations from which a healthy relationship has the potential to grow.

Handling disagreements

Disagreements are a part of normal life, even in a healthy relationship. It is how we deal with arguments that is important — not the fact that we have them. Many people new at intimate relationships behave in unhealthy ways during stressful times such as during an argument, or feel scared that their partner will cheat on them or leave them. You may have seen your mother yell and throw things, or your father use threats and name-calling. Under stress you may find yourself repeating these behaviours with your partners. It is what happens next that is the difference between a potentially healthy or unhealthy partner. A healthy enough person will see where their behaviour was out of line and be able to own it, talk about it and make changes for the better.

Unhealthy partners do not change and grow. They deflect and blame. They do not have the emotional capacity to take responsibility for their behaviour or even care about the impact of their behaviour on others. They prefer to have power and control over another person to feel better about themselves. Unhealthy people also lack empathy and the ability to really care about another person. Most commonly this is because they weren't cared for in a healthy way themselves when growing up and possibly had a parent who was controlling, aggressive or violent. They may have also been severely bullied and rejected by their peers.

Unresolved past rejections and hurt cause feelings such as frustration, jealousy or anger, which can make unhealthy people feel vulnerable and powerless. This is why unhealthy people can become aggravated or dangerous in some situations — because they are unable to manage the uncomfortable feelings that remind them of the past. They become abusive to control the situation, and therefore their uncomfortable feelings.

If it is you who gets ugly by lashing out or blaming others when these fear-based emotions come up, what should you do?

Anger almost always comes from fear, from a part of you that feels scared, not good enough or hurt. These feelings cannot hurt you. Feel and accept them by breathing.

BREATHE OUT LOTS, COUNT TO 10, COUNT TO 20. TAKE TIME TO HAVE COMPASSION FOR THE PART OF YOU THAT IS AFRAID AND FEEL THE FEELINGS. SIT WITH THEM AND TAKE THE TIME TO LET THEM COME UP. IN DOING SO THEY CAN BE RELEASED AND THEREFORE LOSE THEIR CHARGE.

It's when they are pushed down (repressed), or covered up by anger or distractions such as texting, arguing, alcohol, sex and drugs, that they stay locked in place, holding you and others hostage.

SIX RULES THAT HELP WHEN DISAGREEMENTS ARISE:

1. The Golden Rule — treat others as you like to be treated.

2. Stay focused on the problem at hand (don't bring up old issues).

3. Avoid extreme fighting — giving ultimatums and 'all or nothing' statements.

4. Try not to displace your anger at someone else onto your partner.

5. Avoid passive-aggressive behaviour — indirect and sneaky expressions of anger.

6. Instead try the straightforward approach of saying 'I am angry at you for such and such'.

People unwittingly get caught up in unhealthy relationships because of the subtle nature of behaviour that erodes their sense of personal power, which is often a confusing mixture of manipulation, excitement and charm. Some relationships begin intensely with boundaries set by the unhealthy partner. This intensity is often labelled as love, when it is not love; it is a form of control. This might be characterised by excessive texting, questioning, spending all your time together, or games such as those Weatherston played with Sophie. He expected her to chase him while being charming one day but abusive the next. In the face of such behaviour, mixed in with the rush of a new relationship, it is understandable how it becomes easy for those involved to justify, forgive or excuse it.

Very few people are equipped with the skills to spot an unhealthy partner before put-downs and emotional manipulation take their toll. Very quickly people can begin to believe they are not worthy or are at fault, just as Sophie did. This often makes them more dependent on the unhealthy partner for approval and love. The Sophie Elliott Foundation is working to change these perceptions. You now have available to you more knowledge and understanding of the complexity of relationships so that you can identify and choose healthy partners and healthy relationships.

How do we have lasting, healthy relationships?

You are probably not going to find your life partner while still at school, and you probably wouldn't want to! But at the end of the day, human beings have a deep desire to couple up, and in today's world people will likely have somewhere between two and 10 relationships of three months or more before they are 25 years old. Young people should regard each relationship they embark on as a 'practice run'.

WHEN YOU ARE IN A RELATIONSHIP, CONSIDER THE FOLLOWING QUESTIONS:

1. Does this person make me happy?

2. Will they support me to achieve my goals?

3. Do I feel safe?

What would it mean to have a great long-term relationship? What if we took the pressure off needing relationships to be long-term and just focused on them being great, letting the long-term sort itself out? What does a great relationship mean to you? Fun, safe, supportive and intimate? Once again it comes back to you, the individual. You have a choice to lighten up and enjoy finding out about the person you are in a relationship with. What is important is how you handle the uncomfortable feelings and how you communicate them, especially during times of conflict and stress.

Respectful communication between partners is the biggest key to healthy relationships. Owning what is ours, how we feel or what we think, and communicating in a non-blaming or attacking way, may take a bit to master. But by doing this we give a loving, respectful relationship a chance to grow.

Loving feelings and connection start to die when we don't communicate.

The four Rs

The difference between a relationship becoming more connected or less connected, healthy (equal) or unhealthy (controlling), is how negative feelings are handled.

The four Rs are a way of understanding how loving feelings can fade in relationships. 'Pushed down' feelings of annoyance and resentment, if not worked through, can eventually shut down loving feelings towards a partner. The identified levels of feelings people go through before the love fades completely are Resistance, Resentment, Rejection and Repression. John Gray, author of *Men Are From Mars, Women Are From Venus,* describes them as follows:

Resistance — *Annoyance* — You feel annoyed (or other negative emotion) at how your partner behaves; you feel annoyed but you don't say anything.

Resentment — *Pissed off* — Your partner continues the challenging behaviour, bringing up negative feelings in you that build up over time and become feelings of resentment.

Rejection — *Piss off* — Resentment blocks out loving feelings and if you continue to ignore and not deal with the challenging behaviour, then you will most probably find you will want to reject your partner in some way.

Repression — *Who cares* — Avoiding conflict leads to people repressing (pushing down) their feelings instead of communicating their feelings and needs. This can create a relationship that is disconnected and lacking in emotional and physical connection.

Varying degrees of conflict, insecurities or other stressors are a part of all relationships. It is how we and our partners handle these stressful moments that is important. If abuse comes into these moments of stress, then foundations of trust and respect are eroded. In a healthy relationship we care about our partner hearing our point of view because we care about them. We want them to hear and understand us. Through this two-way relationship of listening and caring about each other, understanding, acceptance, trust and love grow over time. Trust and love cannot grow in a relationship that is controlling and abusive.

Scenarios

Ask yourself these questions:

- ✿ How long have I been in this relationship?
- ✿ How much has been good and how much not so good?
- ✿ What has the last month been like?

> Were there lots of put-downs, being
> ignored, used for sex, or taken for
> granted?

If you answer yes to the last question, then this is the other person showing their true colours. This is who they really are and, in all likelihood, this is probably as good as it gets.

When a relationship is equal it is more like a good solid friendship, where both partners want to be together, support each other and there is no element of power and control. It is only in this type of relationship that you will feel safe enough to express your true self, which is what we all want and deserve. To love and be loved.

Consider the following scenarios and think about the questions posed; or go through each scenario with friends.

Scenario 1

Marty gets moody. His dad does too, and doesn't talk to anyone for days. Marty finds himself acting the same way. His girlfriend pushes and pushes him to talk though; she messes with his head, she is the reason he gets so dark.

✿ Who needs to speak up for their boundaries? Why?

✿ What could they say to explain how it feels when their partner acts that way?

✿ What is the worst possible outcome?

✿ What is the best possible outcome?

Scenario 2

Luke and Madelyn have been neighbours for years. They started going out six months ago and things have been pretty intense. Lately Luke has been losing his temper over little things and doing scary things like smashing his fist into the wall beside Madelyn and sometimes pinning her down and yelling at her. Madelyn really loves Luke and thinks that it is okay, because he would never hit her.

✿ Who needs to speak up for their boundaries? Why?

✿ What could they say to explain how it feels when their partner acts that way?

✿ What is the worst possible outcome?

✿ What is the best possible outcome?

Scenario 3

Liz and Teena have been a couple for over a year. Teena gets really iffy over Liz's other friends and her family. Liz feels that Teena just wants her to see no one but her. They have lots of fun, but sometimes Teena seems she is seconds away from being moody — making Liz feel confused and annoyed that she has to always be so careful of upsetting Teena.

❀ Who needs to speak up for their boundaries? Why?

❀ What could they say to explain how it feels when their partner acts that way?

❀ What is the worst possible outcome?

❀ What is the best possible outcome?

Scenario 4

Hannah has started to see Scott; he is five years older than her and really hot! He is a bit mean and moody at times, and sometimes doesn't contact Hannah for a whole weekend. She gets so upset and confused, but then he can be so sweet when he does get in touch — as long as she doesn't question him.

❀ Who needs to speak up for their boundaries? Why?

❀ What could they say to explain how

> it feels when their partner acts that
> way?
> ❀ What is the worst possible outcome?
> ❀ What is the best possible outcome?

Scenario 5

Gretchen has been seeing Joe for three months. Joe is hot, sweet and fun. He can get a bit insecure though, so Gretchen has stopped going out so much and makes sure he doesn't see her talking to other guys, because he sulks for days.

> ❀ Who needs to speak up for their
>   boundaries? Why?
> ❀ What could they say to explain how
>   it feels when their partner acts that
>   way?
> ❀ What is the worst possible outcome?
> ❀ What is the best possible outcome?

Scenario 6

Mike and Nicole have been going out for over a year. Nicole feels she doesn't love Mike any more and wants to break up. Each time she has brought it up in the past he has gotten really upset and threatened to kill himself if she leaves him.

- ✿ Who needs to speak up for their boundaries? Why?
- ✿ What could they say to explain how it feels when their partner acts that way?
- ✿ What is the worst possible outcome?
- ✿ What is the best possible outcome?

Scenario 7

Lewis and Mel have been together forever. They are mostly good, but they fight a lot, and it can get ugly pretty quickly. They scream at each other and smash things. They have both been violent towards each other too. They both love each other, but when it's bad, it's pretty bad.

- ✿ Who needs to speak up for their boundaries? Why?
- ✿ What could they say to explain how it feels when their partner acts that way?
- ✿ What is the worst possible outcome?
- ✿ What is the best possible outcome?

CHAPTER 9

Mirror, Mirror on the Wall

What do you want out of a relationship? Sometimes it's good to make a plan when you are rational and calm and free from an emotional relationship hang-up. Below are two lists — one contains the behaviours and attitudes you might find in a healthy, equal relationship and the other contains those from a relationship that is unhealthy or controlling.

On the blank pages that follow take time when you are calm to list the things in a relationship that are important to you. If, when you enter a relationship, you feel things aren't as you expected, look at what you wrote when your head and heart were clear. Compare it with what you are experiencing now.

IN A HEALTHY FRIENDSHIP/ RELATIONSHIP, YOU:

Treat each other with respect

Feel comfortable with each other

Are not violent with each other

Can forgive and get over conflicts

Enjoy the time you spend together

Support one another equally

Take interest in one another's lives: health, family, interests, etc.

Can trust each other

Communicate clearly and openly with clear boundaries

Make healthy decisions about alcohol or other drugs

Encourage other friendships

Know that most people in your life are happy about the friendship

Have more good times in the friendship than bad

Respect each other's belongings

Have the freedom to do your own thing

IN AN UNHEALTHY FRIENDSHIP/ RELATIONSHIP, ONE OR BOTH OF YOU:

Try to control or manipulate the other person

Make the other person feel bad about themselves

Use put-downs or call the other person names, even as a joke

Do not make time for each other

Criticise the other person's friends

Are afraid of the other person's moods or temper

Discourage the other person from being close to anyone else

Ignore each other when one is speaking or use the silent treatment

Are overly possessive or get jealous about other friendships

Push, grab, hit, punch, or throw objects

Talk about the other person, or pass on things said in confidence

Use threats or guilt trips to get their own way

Get angry or jealous when the other person spends time with others

WHO AM I — WHAT DO
I EXPECT FROM RELATIONSHIPS?

WHO AM I — WHAT AM I GETTING FROM MY CURRENT RELATIONSHIP?

CHAPTER 10

One for the Boys

By Nigel Latta

Relationships are complicated things. I'd like to tell all you young men out there that they get easier as you get older, but unfortunately that simply isn't the case. Relationships change in all kinds of interesting and unexpected ways, but they don't get easier.

When you're young you think the hardest thing in the world is getting *in* to a relationship in the first place, and that once you are in it, it will all be much easier. Which makes complete sense at one level, but is also completely wrong. Getting in to a relationship is nothing compared to the complexity of actually *staying* in a relationship.

That may not be what you want to hear, but it's true. If you think talking to girls is hard, try finding one you can happily talk to for the next 20, 30 or even 70 years.

That's hard.

Worth doing, don't get me wrong, but hard.

Personally, I think the best relationship advice I ever heard was from a couple in Hamilton, Ray and Peg, who'd been married for 70 years. When I asked them for their top three tips on staying together they looked a little puzzled at first — mainly because I think they were from a generation which learned to think before bullet points were invented — and then Peg said: 'I guess you just have to keep busy, and don't hold a grudge.'

Good advice.

This book is full of good advice as well, to help you navigate the process of beginning and maintaining healthy relationships, and if you take the time to read it, and to think about what it's saying, then you'll have a much happier time. In the first part of the book Lesley Elliott talks about the signs of an unhealthy relationship, and in the previous chapter Gayna McConnell describes how we sometimes find ourselves sliding into bad relationships without really noticing it until we're in so deep that it can seem hard to know how to get out. She has some great strategies about how to maintain boundaries, keep your sense of self and how to deal with disagreements or abusive people.

In this chapter I'm going to talk about something no one ever talks about. We should — because we've known about it for over 30 years — but we don't.

Blood and broken plates

I want to talk to you about something that might challenge everything you think you know about violence in intimate relationships, and to do that I want to tell you a story. About a million years ago, when I was a student at Otago University, I spent some of my weekends as a volunteer ambulance officer. What can I say . . . I just liked the lights and sirens and all the excitement. One night we were called out to a domestic dispute. I remember that it was amazingly cold and we had to be careful not to slip on the concrete path leading into the house because ice was already starting to form.

When we got inside we found a man with a major cut on his head sitting in the middle of the lounge surrounded by blood and shattered crockery. An argument had broken out and his partner had thrown a plate at his head with remarkable accuracy given they were both drunk and she was clearly very angry. As we bandaged him up it emerged that this happened a lot. They would argue, his partner would get angry, and she would 'lash out'.

It wasn't his first trip to the hospital.

We took him to A&E. She travelled in the back with us, and I remember thinking that she was a really angry person. She wasn't really doing anything physical then, but it was like a great brooding cloud surrounded her. I was glad to get her out of the ambulance and away from me. When I last saw them she was sitting beside him in a cubicle waiting for the doctor . . . still with the ugly angry cloud hanging over them both. We didn't call the police, and the hospital didn't either.

And why not?

Because, in the eyes of the world at that time — and sadly, in many cases, still today as well — it wasn't *real* domestic violence. It was 'just' an argument which had got out of hand. She'd lost her rag and clocked him with a plate. It would only have been domestic violence if he had hit her.

Right?

Wrong.

Uncomfortable truths

When we think about domestic violence we always think of it in the same way: the man is always the offender — the perpetrator — and the woman is always the victim. There's a good reason for that, mainly because these tend to be the only cases we hear about.

Obviously tragedies such as Sophie Elliott's murder touch all of us, and bring the issue of violence directed at young women into sharp focus. It was very clear in that instance, as her mother Lesley Elliott details earlier in this book, that Clayton Weatherston was a violent and controlling man. He utilised a number of tactics in his abuse of Sophie that were deliberate, manipulative and calculated.

Her death, at his hands, was a tragedy that is beyond words.

But as Lesley has described very clearly, there were a number of warning signs that he was an abusive man. No one could possibly have predicted that he would murder Sophie, but if she had known more about how power and control tactics are used by abusers, then she may have realised sooner that Weatherston was bad news, and she may have ended the relationship much sooner. That's the reason Lesley started the Sophie Elliott Foundation, and wrote this book, so that other young people can learn more about what bad relationships look like, and get out before they get hurt.

What's important for all you young men to understand, though, is that the advice and information contained in this book applies to you just as it does to young women. It is not okay to hurt young women you are in relationships with, but it is also not okay for you to be hurt by them either.

Who hurts who?

It might surprise you to learn that there have been over 200 studies since the 1970s that have found that, when it comes to violence within intimate relationships, men and women are both victims and perpetrators in equal amounts. It's important to understand that this doesn't mean that in an abusive relationship the man and the woman contribute to the violence equally. What it means is that men are just as likely to be the victims of violence in a relationship as women are.

We used to believe that if women were violent in relationships that this was predominantly in self-defence, and at a far lesser level. Research clearly shows us that this is not true. Women can be just as violent as men, using all the same strategies of power and control, and with similar levels of force. This statement seems to go against everything that we know about violence in relationships, but in reality it's only going against everything we *think* we know.

Sophie Elliott was murdered by a violent and controlling male ex-partner. She is one of a long list of women who have lost their lives at the hands of violent and controlling men. Yet just as tragically, guys are also murdered by *their* violent and controlling *female* ex-partners. Men, and young men as well, are also subjected to unhealthy and dysfunctional relationships; we just don't talk about them. Instead we talk about guys solely as the bad guys. Violence is only ever stuff that we do, not what gets done to us.

Well, it does get done to us.

And it's not okay.

Re-read this book

So knowing all that, I'd suggest you go back and have another look at the advice and information contained in this book. It's for *all* young people, and this includes young men as well. There may well be some young men who will read this book and recognise unhealthy things they might be doing to their girlfriend. If they do, then I sincerely hope they decide to get some help, and reach out to someone — maybe a parent, a school guidance counsellor, or Youthline — to get that help.

Help is there, you just need to ask.

It might also be that there are some young men who read this book and recognise unhealthy things their girlfriend is doing *to* them. If they do, then I hope those young men will reach out for help as well. Talk to someone you trust. That could be a parent, someone at school, a friend's parent . . . anyone. You don't need to know what to do, you just need to reach out to someone.

It's not okay for you to hurt someone, and it's also not okay for someone to hurt you. So re-read this book and, as you do, remember this one simple truth:

VIOLENCE, IN ANY FORM, IS NOT OKAY. EVER.

CHAPTER II

Friends

After Sophie died I immersed myself in trying to understand the issue of violence, especially in a dating relationship. How did Sophie get into this situation? Why couldn't she get out of something that was so obviously bad? How could she, and I for that matter, have failed to see the signs of an abusive and controlling relationship? And why, when I told Sophie that she was always moaning about Weatherston and should leave him, did she minimise or defend his behaviour as 'not that bad'?

I've done a lot of research and talked to many profes-sionals who work in the field of abuse prevention. More importantly, I've talked to countless men and women who have been abused or who were abusers. What I'm going to relate in this chapter are simply my observations and some sound advice school guidance counsellors have provided me with. I urge young men and women caught up in abusive situations to seek help — talk to someone, be it parents, friends, counsellors or an adult you trust. There are heaps of organisations in the community which can give good advice, like Women's Refuge, Rape Crisis or the various help lines. There are contact details for these organisations on page 157. In the case of online abuse, organisations like NetSafe could be the right one to contact. Rather than provide solutions, what I want to do is raise issues, things that you and your friends might like to think about. I hope it helps.

Wolves in sheep's clothing

I believe you can often tell what someone might be like by looking at the people around them. Choosing a boyfriend, girlfriend or long-term partner is never easy. A sign that a relationship may become negative or possibly destructive can lie in what your partner's peer group does for fun. Are they into going to parties, getting pissed and having sex?

Ask yourself, what are their friends like? What is their attitude towards their family? Do they respect their mothers, fathers, sisters and brothers, or others in the group? Perhaps another key indicator is your partner's attitude to animals. For instance, Clayton Weatherston had a cat, and he lived in an apartment high up on a steep hill with a drop from the balcony to the ground below. Sophie was most upset when he once threatened to throw his cat over the balcony. While he didn't, Sophie had taken him seriously. She loved cats, especially her beloved Kade, and was quite upset at his threat. There is a strong link between cruelty to animals and abuse; so much so that the Society for the Prevention of Cruelty to Animals (SPCA) has an agreement with Child, Youth and Family (CYFs). If SPCA officers are called to investigate a case of pet abuse, they will see if children seem safe, and similarly CYFs will also check on pets when they make home visits. That's why I say don't ignore animal cruelty in a partner. It could be a warning sign.

In other cases, if incentives to be with someone include money and gifts, then perhaps ask yourself why. Make a list of the things being offered, and think about if they seem to be over the top. If you feel too pressured or controlled, then it could be worthwhile thinking twice about being in the relationship. Pressure might also come in the form of wanting you to have sex before you feel the relationship is ready. Maybe it's the other person wanting to take control of you by encouraging you to do and be what they want. This could include having to wear clothes the other person likes, or only having friends they approve of and who mightn't even be your friends. Or it could mean you not being allowed any friends of the opposite gender. All these things can lead to a loss of your own identity.

There are ways to sort out the wolves in sheep's clothing by considering who your partner and their friends really are. Is their peer group into sport, healthy activities, youth groups, community events, in jobs or training courses? Or they may be into other pursuits such as dancing, playing in a band, or have an interest in art. Also consider how adults relate to them.

At the Sophie Elliott Foundation we have a lot of experts and professionals who advise us from time to time. One such person is Dr Alison Towns. Alison is a clinical psychologist in Auckland who has studied the topic of relationship violence extensively and has written several papers about it. One is called *The Cultures of Cool and Being a Man: Getting in Early to Prevent Domestic Abuse.* Another paper of hers that I have read is *The Cultures of Cool: Getting in Early to Prevent Domestic Violence.* The first paper's focus was to interview a lot of young men and the second, written in collaboration with Hazel Scott, took the woman's viewpoint. What I want to do here is illustrate the points I'm making with three short interviews from the second paper from a young woman's perspective. Although these examples are comments by girls, I want to make it quite clear that power and control comes from both boys and girls.

I kind of just lost my life and I
kind of realised I just didn't have
anything else to do. I hadn't seen
my friends for ages and I couldn't
even dress the way I wanted and
over a period of about eight months
he even became slightly violent
towards me as well. Things like . . .
because we started living together
after about six months, and things
like . . . if his friends came over
and I didn't sort of get the beers or
something like that, like a domestic
little girl, he would yell at me and
maybe throw something at me when
he was drunk and then he'd always
apologise and so it would be okay
and we'd get back together and stuff.
It's like when someone starts to tell
you stuff about yourself you think . . .
well shit . . . this is my boyfriend and
he's supposed to love me and he's
saying these nasty things about me,
that you kind of start to believe them
because this person is supposed to be
the closest to you out of everyone. He
must know me and he starts to say
these horrible things, and you believe
them and you just keep getting lower
and lower, and it took me ages to
realise that and then it resulted in

having to get a restraining order
against him, and like it was the worst
case scenario.

Well I was controlled in every shape.
I wasn't allowed to go anywhere, say
anything, see anyone, think anything,
do anything. Wasn't allowed to do
anything that wasn't in his little rule
book which changed all the time.

It got to the point where if I wanted
to hang out with my sister, he used to
get jealous and get angry and told me
I looked like a slut if I wore tops that
were low-cut or a little bit too tight.
I was a slut and if we were walking
past people and a guy would walk
past, and I wouldn't even see him,
he would just say . . . are you going
to sleep with him? . . . and I would
go what? . . . and he'd go . . . you're
just a little slut.

Then there are Jekyll and Hyde characters who may
not be so easy to spot. On the one hand they can be
friendly, charismatic and outgoing. But when you
are alone they become agitated, anxious, controlling
and verbally abusive. You don't get to see this side
until you get to know them a bit more. This is a big

alarm bell that perhaps this relationship will not be good for you.

Isolation and secrecy

Other key indicators of an unsafe relationship can be isolation and secrecy. Isolation can come about because of secrecy, often because your parents or friends don't approve of the relationship and you keep it secret. Once you are in the relationship and become isolated you are kind of stuck. You can find yourself quickly out of your depth and with no support — it's a difficult situation to deal with.

Isn't it better to question why the relationship has to be kept secret? Isn't this in itself an indication that things aren't going well? Are you being asked to do things that you know your parents wouldn't approve of? If a relationship can't withstand the question 'why?' then there is a problem.

Isolation can lead to very serious problems. If you become isolated from friends and family, who can you turn to when things really do go wrong? Signs to watch out for include the other person in the relationship determining who you will see, to a point where you virtually have to ask permission. This is a particularly controlling way to behave. If everything is decided for you, that no one else is important and you must only live to please your partner, then take this as a big warning bell.

Real friends

Humans seem to be awfully good at ignoring gut instinct. Sometimes we over-think the situation or make excuses for the behaviour of others. On reflection, I know Sophie did. It seems to be standard practice for younger people to go through denial and minimisation. Our brains tend to justify situations and we tell ourselves, 'It's not actually as bad as that.' Self-blame, denial and minimisation are the things that stop us listening to the warning bells. And the warning bells don't have to be massive. Often the accumulation of small things put together, that might seem to be of little consequence on their own, could show a dominant pattern of behaviour.

Some people have an ally or a go-to person. Who are your allies? Having a list of possible allies could be a good strategy.

In Chapter 6 I spoke about bystanders and how others overheard an argument between Sophie and Weatherston that turned violent. No one intervened. Even worse, I've heard of cases where people are not only passive bystanders but actively encourage unsafe behaviour. For instance, take the scenario of a group of girls at a party — one of them becomes quite drunk and ends up in a bedroom with a boy. Instead of intervening to check on their friend's wellbeing, the other girls lock the door. They regard this as funny until things turn ugly.

Real friends are important. So much can happen in a group setting where behaviour is often peer driven. I think it's important to know who your girlfriend or boyfriend really is, as well as your other friends, by looking at their values, interests, pastimes, what they do in their spare time and what they want to do with their lives.

Peer groups can be lifesavers. If you get drunk your friends shouldn't lock you in a room and laugh; if they are real friends they will help you out. Just as they won't let you get into a car with a drunk driver. A good friend will pull you back and save you from making mistakes.

Go-to people

If you think something's not okay, your gut instinct will tell you. This is where a hierarchy of people to talk to could be helpful. A peer group usually comes first. Talking face to face with mates to check out something that feels weird or unsafe could be number one on your list. Some people have an ally or a go-to person. Who are your allies? Having a list of possible allies could be a good strategy. These people could be anyone who can give you good, sound advice. I was fortunate because Sophie confided in me, so for you it may be your mother, aunt, sister, grandmother, father, friend or close neighbour — anyone who can relate to what you are experiencing and who knows you. In a culture of silence we seldom get this other person's voice checking out if we are okay.

A list of things to make a situation clearer might include:

✿ Trusting my gut feelings.
✿ Checking it out. Is the situation real or imagined?
✿ Is it me or the other person causing the problems in this relationship?
✿ Keep talking about issues and carefully choose who I talk to.

The practical advice and skills in this book are some things you might use to keep yourself safe as you negotiate the world of relationships. I absolutely believe that had Sophie had relationship advice when she was at high school she would have been better equipped to deal with the situation she became caught in. I then wouldn't be in the position I am today. I hope that what I have written and the information in the Loves-Me-Not programme will be of help.

At this point I want to reinforce something that I feel is important. I'm sure that by and large most relationships are happy, healthy and fun to be in. I know all of Sophie's relationships were really good, up until the last one. So I say to you, enjoy being with your boyfriend or girlfriend but be aware of the signs Sophie and I missed. I hope you never get to see those signs, but if they ever do come along you will now be able to recognise them.

Conclusion

Looking back, the signs
Sophie and I missed now
seem glaringly obvious
— yet we both missed
them. I've rationalised
that if we couldn't see the
signs, many other people
will not know what is
happening, let alone take
affirmative action.

So what were the effects of Weatherston's behaviour towards Sophie?

She very quickly became depressed, anxious and worried. I initially put this down to the workload she was carrying. After secondary school she spent four years at university and wanted to get on with the next stage of her life as a graduate analyst for Treasury in Wellington. She was completing an honours degree as well as a dissertation, and being a perfectionist, as many young people are, burdened herself with the pressure of trying to achieve the best possible outcome from her work.

Added to this was a part-time job, a busy social life and a boyfriend who was screwing around with her head. This left Sophie with the feeling that she was out of control, to the stage she believed she was going crazy.

Weatherston's constant put-downs led to her feeling ashamed that she wasn't good enough. In fact, she took the blame for him treating her as he did, believing that if she was a better person or had a better appearance he wouldn't treat her that way. She ended up hating her body.

> MY ADVICE TO YOUNG PEOPLE IS TO BE YOURSELF — *YOU* DON'T HAVE TO CHANGE. IF A PERSON TRULY LIKES YOU, IT IS FOR WHO YOU ARE. IF THEY WANT YOU TO CHANGE THEN YOU HAVE TO ASK YOURSELF, 'IS THEIR ATTENTION GENUINE?'

Get help

The biggest effect, however, was the day Sophie came home one afternoon in floods of tears yet again and said, 'Doesn't he know I have low self-esteem?' This comment blew me away. I was very close to Sophie and in no way did I ever suspect she had a low opinion of herself. But that's what this insidious cycle of behaviour led her to believe. I said, 'I can't help you any more. You need to talk to a professional.'

I'd been a listening post, but this was getting more serious. We talked about possible counsellors and Sophie was adamant she couldn't go to Student Health as he worked at the university and it was sure to get around. Despite my assurances that confidentiality was paramount, Sophie insisted she wouldn't go. I said I would find someone through my work. Within a couple of days Sophie came home and said, 'Have you found that counsellor yet?' I told her I hadn't but would get on to it and she said, 'It doesn't matter — I've made an appointment with Student Health.' I knew then that Sophie had accepted things were getting serious.

Sophie visited the counsellor twice and came home and told me all that had been said. On the second visit the counsellor said, 'I don't think it's you who has problems. I think this man has issues.' Sophie left it at that.

After Sophie died I found the counsellor's business card in her bedside drawer. On it the counsellor had written, 'Get back to me when you are home from Aus.' As I've mentioned, when Sophie came back from her trip to Australia she was refreshed and relaxed. The relationship with Weatherston was well over and she was excited about the future. There was no need to go back to the counsellor.

After I found the card I had a burning desire to meet the counsellor, so I emailed her. To this day I have no idea why I wanted to do this. Perhaps it was a 'connecting' thing.

The counsellor eventually decided to meet with me and said she would have someone with her and I was also welcome to bring someone. I went alone and spent a good half hour telling the counsellor what Sophie had relayed to me and what had been said back. The counsellor nodded and at the end we all had a hug and a cry and as I walked down the street it dawned on me that the counsellor hadn't told me any more than I already knew, even though I'm sure she knew more. And I really respected her for that. Although Sophie was no longer with us, the counsellor kept Sophie's confidentiality.

Don't ever be afraid to ask for help, because you may not have been the first person to be abused by your partner.

I mention it here to give young people the confidence to seek out help. Professional counsellors are there for you and they will ensure your privacy is secure, so I implore young people facing the sort of confusion Sophie was subjected to, to please seek help.

Find someone to talk to. Through my travels around the country and visiting schools I see many caring guidance counsellors. If this is not for you, talk to a close friend, relative or special person in your life — someone who can guide you. There are plenty of agencies out there specifically designed to help, whether it be one with a teen focus like

Youthline, or broader agencies like Women's Refuge or Rape Crisis. You don't have to be raped to seek help, nor do you have to be living with someone or have kids with them to approach a refuge. They have excellent programmes to help anyone in an abusive relationship. They don't just run refuges. And Women's Refuge even has support programmes for males. Whatever you do, my advice is to seek help and hopefully this is a lesson from the Loves-Me-Not programme that you will take with you.

Police districts each have a family violence co-ordinator and a team of officers specially trained and committed to dealing with the issues of family violence and abuse. They recognise the role of psychological abuse in relationships. From what I have read and seen, New Zealand is well served in this regard.

Don't ever be afraid to ask for help, because you may not have been the first person to be abused by your partner. We found that Sophie wasn't the first to be abused by Weatherston. Yet for a variety of reasons not one of his previous girlfriends had reported him — and Sophie didn't either. In fact, if Sophie hadn't got in his way he might still be working at Otago University and getting into relationships that would probably have followed the same patterns as his others.

Respect each other

If I learnt anything from Sophie's brief relationship (and it was only five months), it was the need to respect each other. I believe any relationship, be it boyfriend or girlfriend, workplace, friendships, sporting or other, needs to contain good levels of mutual respect, trust, tolerance and informed choices. And this goes both ways.

When addressing girls' schools I pose the question, 'Have you thought about how you expect your boyfriend to treat you and how you treat him?' Both parties have to share the respect and tolerance. It's no good one person being abusive, or nasty or bitchy, and expecting their partner to be nice in return. Basically it's common decency and common sense.

Don't be fooled into thinking that abusive partners only come from a lower socio-economic group. Abuse crosses all boundaries, and in the past few years I have read, heard or seen plenty of evidence to know it comes from every stratum in society.

Take Weatherston as an example. He wasn't a druggie or a gang member. He came from a middle-class family. He was dux of his high school and was well educated. He had a PhD. But he was still a murderer.

I proudly wear a white ribbon and believe fervently in the White Ribbon campaign. It's essentially men supporting men, blokes standing up and taking responsibility. I know abuse of males by females does go on, but the sad and irrefutable fact is that 85% of reported domestic abuse is perpetrated by males.

From my viewpoint I pose the question, 'What would you do if you were in a relationship and didn't feel happy or safe?' My first response is always dump him or her. There are plenty of nice people out there and my advice is to find someone who loves and respects you rather than continually antagonises you and puts you down.

When addressing girls' schools I pose the question, 'Have you thought about how you expect your boyfriend to treat you and how you treat him?' Both parties have to share the respect and tolerance.

You or your family don't want to be standing in our shoes. Take my advice — if your relationship feels unsafe, it probably is. Get out of it. If you suffer abuse, even psychological, talk to someone. Seek help. Do something about it.

LOOK FOR THE SIGNS — THE SORT OF SIGNS SOPHIE AND I MISSED. IF THE CLASSIC ONES OF THREATS, LACK OF EMPATHY, SEXUAL ISSUES,

> UNHEALTHY COMMUNICATION, PHYSICAL
> ABUSE, POWER AND CONTROL OR
> ERRATIC BEHAVIOUR START TO SET
> ALARM BELLS RINGING, LISTEN
> TO THEM AND ACT ON THEM.

In conclusion I want to dedicate what I have written to my beloved daughter, Sophie. I hope that by sharing the hard lessons I have learned it will help other young people to extricate themselves from unhealthy relationships. Better still, I hope my words will prevent some young people from getting into those situations in the first place.

Let me leave you with a quote. When President Obama was in England in 2011, his wife Michelle visited Oxford University and spoke to a gathering of girls from a nearby school. During question time after her speech she said these words:

> 'REACH FOR PARTNERS THAT MAKE
> YOU BETTER.
>
> DO NOT BRING PEOPLE INTO YOUR
> LIFE THAT WEIGH YOU DOWN.

> ## TRUST YOUR INSTINCTS.
> ## GOOD RELATIONSHIPS FEEL GOOD, THEY
> ## FEEL RIGHT. THEY DON'T HURT AND THEY
> ## ARE NOT PAINFUL.'

I couldn't agree more.

Where to go for help

Family Planning www.familyplanning.org.nz
Lifeline www.lifeline.org.nz
NetSafe www.netsafe.org.nz
Rape Crisis www.rpe.co.nz
Women's Refuge www.womensrefuge.org.nz
Youthline www.youthline.co.nz

Zonta International District 16

Through the generosity of Zonta International District 16, as part of their biennium project for 2014–16 supporting the Sophie Elliott Foundation, this book has been made available free of charge to all students undertaking the Loves-Me-Not programme.

Zonta is an international organisation of business and professional women working together to advance the status of women and girls through service and advocacy. There are 28 Zonta Clubs in New Zealand spread from Northland to Otago.

To find out more about Zonta or enquire about membership, visit the District 16 website: www.zonta.org.nz or Zonta International: www.zonta.org

 Zonta International
District 16
Advancing the Status of Women Worldwide

For more information about our titles visit
www.randomhouse.co.nz